Born American

A Chinese Woman's Dream of Liberty

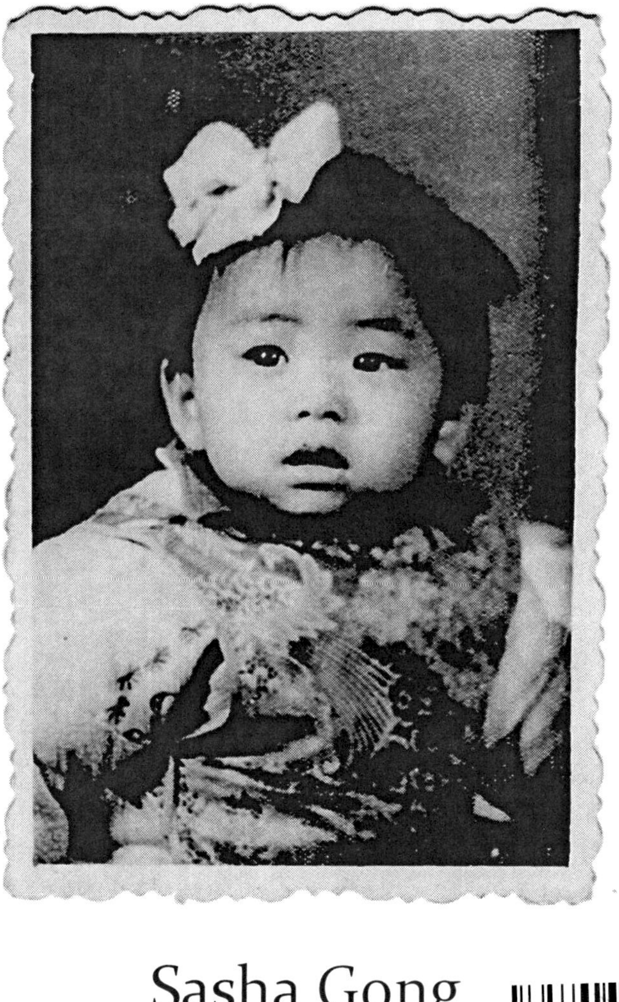

Sasha Gong

NIMBLE BOOKS LLC

NIMBLE BOOKS LLC

Nimble Books LLC

1521 Martha Ave.

Ann Arbor, MI, USA 48103

http://www.NimbleBooks.com

wfz@nimblebooks.com

+1.734-330-2593

Last saved 6/23/2009 3:46 PM

Printed in the United States of America

ISBN-13: 978-1-934840-90-0

ISBN-10: 1-934840-90-4

∞ The paper used in this publication meets the minimum requirements of the American National Standard for Information Sciences—Permanence of Paper for Printed Library Materials, ANSI Z39.48-1992. The paper is acid-free and lignin-free.

Table of Contents

To my grandma Tan Yuegui, who passed on our heritage to me, and to Crystal Luo, who gives me hope for the future.

Hope, faith, & country.

FOREWORD

By Anne Thurston

Born American will warm the heart of every American who reads it. It is the story of Sasha Gong's long journey home.

Sasha was born not in the United States but in China, and she arrived there during a time of great economic and political distress. In the three years after her birth in 1956, a massive, politically induced famine left upwards of 30 million Chinese people dead. Several years later, communist party Chairman Mao Zedong launched the disastrous Great Proletarian Cultural Revolution, a massive, decade-long political campaign that turned millions of China's most talented and potentially productive citizens into enemies of the state.

Sasha knew early that something was terribly wrong, though she was encouraged in the beginning to believe that she must be part of the problem.

Sasha's mother was not merely cold but cruel, constantly portraying her daughter as ugly and unwanted, punishing her for every failure to play by impossible rules. Her mother took special pride in her own adherence to political propriety, which included the persecution of friends and colleagues who failed to adhere to the party's norms. Sasha grew up to the story of the important role her mother had played in the political destruction of student activist Lin Xiling during Mao's devastating 1957 anti-rightist campaign. Lin Xiling was among the most famous of China's student activists to be jailed as a rightist then. She spent 22 years in prison. Years later, when Sasha, too, had become a political activist, the mother turned against her own daughter. It was Sasha's mother who delivered her daughter's personal writings to the authorities, declaring that Sasha had had "political problems" from the time she was three years old.

Sasha's mother was right. Her daughter's rebellion, against parents, teachers, and finally the state, began young. Curious, energetic, and ferociously smart, Sasha was forced by parents and teachers alike into a conformity that she was soon unable to bear. Life, both at home and at school, was a prison. But obedience, Sasha tells us, was just not part of her make-up. By kindergarten, she was already resisting the afternoon nap and "collective poop" that had the entire class sitting on potties for half an hour each day. Called often to task for her repeated transgressions, Sasha knew early that the harsh punishments she received did not fit her childhood crimes. When she seized the opportunity to run away from kindergarten, Sasha realized she was trapped. There was no safe place to go. But the rebel in her had been born.

In 1968, in the midst of the Cultural Revolution while many of her relatives were in jail, Sasha got a copy of Alexander Solzhenitsyn's *One Day in the Life of Ivan Denisovich*. It was a short book. She finished it in two hours, then read it again--and again. Life in Ivan Denisovich's Siberian labor camp was better than her own young life in China. The inmates ate meat. One of them had a Bible. They could discuss their most private feelings, argue about religion, complain about their treatment. They could even criticize "Old Man Whiskers," who, she discovered in a footnote, was none other than Stalin himself. In China, people could be executed for mere slips of the tongue about Mao. Sasha almost envied the Soviet inmates their freedom.

Then the thunderbolt hit. If Stalin was responsible for the misery of the Soviet Union, then Mao was responsible for what was happening in China. Sasha's already shaky political faith was shattered. The lonely, empty, powerless twelve-year old girl with no control over her life was transformed into a political dissident. She was both elated and terrified. She kept her new thoughts to herself.

Nearly a decade passed before Sasha found the group of brilliant, daring, kindred political spirits with whom she was finally free to express her most precious political thoughts. She had been thrilled to read *Whither Guangdong* shortly after it was posted publicly in downtown Guangzhou. Written by an underground group that went by the collective name of Li Yizhe, *Whither Guangdong* created a political sensation, presaging Beijing's own Democracy Wall movement of 1978. With membership in the group, Sasha was free at last to be herself. Her new political friends brought a sense community, comradeship and belonging that she had never felt before.

It also brought them all a stint in jail. But for Sasha, spending her 21st birthday in solitary confinement in a makeshift prison on the third floor of a factory warehouse seemed a small price to pay for the discovery that she was not alone.

Released from confinement in March 1978, Sasha was not fully exonerated until February 1979 when the Li Yizhe group were declared heroes for their political courage. It was then that she began studying for the college entrance exams that would be held that July. Some 200,000 young people in Guangdong took the exam that year. Sasha ranked first. She won a place at Peking University, China's most prestigious institution of higher learning.

Sometime during her university studies, Sasha got the idea of coming to the United States.

She had learned something of the marvels of this country as a small child. On the lap of her beloved grandmother, the only truly kind person in her early life, Sasha was regaled with stories of a place called old Gold Mountain, where buildings were tall, the sky was blue, and oranges were plentiful and golden. Sasha was in second grade when she learned that old Gold Mountain was not in China but the United States, where the place is still known today as San Francisco. By then, however, Sasha had been removed from the care of her American-imperialism-loving grandmother. Speaking well of the United States and old Gold Mountain were mistakes that children with politically incorrect grandmothers learned to avoid.

At Beida, as Peking University is called in Chinese, Sasha's interest in the United States was safely revived. China and the United States had recently re-established diplomatic relations. For the first time since 1949, Americans began studying and teaching in China, and Chinese students and scholars were leaving, in even larger numbers, to study in the United States. One of Sasha's American Fulbright professors gave her a copy of Tocqueville's *Democracy in America*. It was the first English-language book she ever read. Another teacher, of English, assigned the Declaration of Independence. Sasha can still recite most of it by heart. Today, she considers two of its sentences to be the most important 55 words in modern history. One of them begins, "We hold these truths to be self-evident, that all men are created equal, that they are endowed by their Creator with certain unalienable rights, that among these are life, liberty and the pursuit of happiness."

Sasha aimed high. She applied to Harvard. In addition to its place on the academic hierarchy, Harvard is also one of several American universities that have been exceptionally receptive to Chinese students who never finished elementary school, who spent years working on farms and in factories and incarcerated in prison, dissidents brilliant and brave who refused to play by the rules. Sasha arrived in Cambridge in April 1987, with a full scholarship. It did not take her long to realize that she had come home.

Sasha would deny that there is much of the extraordinary in her life. The China side of her story, the tragedy of it especially, was *everybody's* story, she says. Perhaps. But her story is still extraordinary. What makes it so unusual is that she refused to abide by the rules, that even as a child she rebelled against the insistent requirement to conform, that she came to her American beliefs, her inexhaustible desire for freedom, while trapped in Mao's China. If courage can be defined as acting on principle even while fearing the consequences, she showed remarkable courage during times when the vast majority of her countrymen did not.

Sasha says that being a citizen of the United States has allowed her to become more Chinese. The more American she becomes the prouder she is of her Chinese heritage, the more she is able to return to its traditional Confucian values. Here in the United States, she says, she can be both American and Chinese. And as everyone who knows her can surely attest, the rebel in her remains, more daring than devout.

Welcome home, Sasha Gong.

ACKNOWLEDGMENTS

In 2009, I decided to run for the Virginia House of Delegates in the 46th district, where approximately one third of residents are immigrants. During the campaign, I have made many speeches before local book clubs, as all political candidates do. Each time, someone in the audience, after listening to my personal stories, asks the same question:

"Have you written a book?"

The answer was yes, I replied, but it might take some time to get it published.

In fact, I had been thinking about writing down my stories from my old country for more than 10 years. Almost every immigrant I have met has some fascinating story to tell. They normally attribute their lives and successes in America at least in part to what they had to endure before they got here. The experience in their old motherland thus merges into mainstream American life and enriches American heritage.

I did jot a few stories down from time to time, but could never find a block of time to do any serious writing until the summer of 2007. My dear friend Scott Seligman, who speaks Mandarin Chinese almost like a native and jokes in Cantonese like a Hong Kong taxi driver, read the first few chapters, and made it his mission to push me to the finish line. He not only edited the entire manuscript, but also coaxed some chapters out of me that I otherwise would have skipped. Driven by Scott, I finished the book in two months.

Through Scott, I met Diane Nine, who has represented many prominent authors in Washington. Diane took on the project and became my book agent. She tells me that I am one of her best clients because I rarely bothered her. I rarely bothered her because I had full confidence in her abilities.

Many friends read the manuscript, and they thoughtfully provided their insights and advice, all of which helped to shape the book further. Among them, I must thank Yoma Ullman, Audrey Lee, Ann Crittenden, Anne Thurston, Sue Bremner, Zhao Li, and Wing Thye Woo.

My very talented young friend Crystal Luo—she was 13 when she read the book – has been my inspiration all along. Born in Minnesota in 1995, Crystal has enjoyed all the best that America can provide—liberty, equality, opportunity, and creativity. She also inherited from her Chinese parents many great traits from that culture, especially from her very devoted mom, my good friend Liu Hong. I have dedicated this book partly to her, because in her I see our future.

Congressman Frank Wolf has been a great mentor to me. As a life-long promoter of human rights and democracy, he encouraged me to publish the book after reading the manuscript. He even wrote a letter to the White House, telling the President about it.

My Aunt Huang Xiuzhu and Uncle Li Pingri provided me with all the old photos. They both suffered a great deal during the Cultural Revolution, but they always retained their inherent goodness and their kindness toward other human beings, and always remained optimistic about the future. My sister Sherry and my brothers James and Sonny shared many of the same experiences and provided different angles for me. Without their contributions, this book would look very different and would, I think, present a much narrower point of view.

I also want to take this opportunity to thank my good friend and campaign manager Doug Brooks. Without his help, I would not be able to spare the time, or find the psychological peace, to finish the final editing of the book.

Last but not least, I must express my gratitude to Bill Drayton, the most important person in my life over the past decade. Bill listened to many chapters while we were watching sea lions along the Nova Scotia seashore and resting along the trails of the Aspen Mountains. He criticized. I argued. Of course I was always right, but I did make some important changes later - quietly.

I have named this book "Born American," even though it is really about my life in China. Born American, to me, means born free, which is the central theme of the book. It is my fond hope that all of mankind will be free in the near future.

Sasha Gong
Falls Church, Virginia
May 28, 2009

PROLOGUE: THE AMERICAN DREAM ... WITH AN ACCENT

Soon after arriving in the United States, I discovered that I had been born an American. It just took me thirty-one years to get here.

It was an interesting journey, though. Bumpy, but interesting.

As happens every now and then, some people are born in the wrong era, and others in the wrong place. Born and raised in the People's Republic of China in the 1950s and 1960s, I never really felt at home there. I had a peculiar feeling that the life I was living did not really belong to me, or that I somehow did not belong to the life that had been assigned to me. My plight was just one of God's careless mistakes, made from time to time at the expense of powerless people like me.

As a consequence, almost from the beginning, I struggled to assimilate, to be a normal person, but without notable success. I tried to please others, to follow the rules and to conform. I made a lot of painful efforts to fit in, but nothing seemed to work. My attempts to achieve an ordinary life—to be one of the neighborhood kids, an average student, a 9-to-5 job holder—all failed rather miserably. No matter what I did, I felt like an outsider in the society into which I was born. As a consequence, I always felt inadequate—never myself, never at home. Psychologically, I remained an outcast—that is, until I finally landed in America.

On top of all of this, I never had much opportunity for normal schooling. When I was nine, my family got into political trouble, which was not all that unusual in China during that era. My grandfather, who was raising my siblings and me, was accused by the Communist Party of being a counterrevolutionary. He lost his job and his urban residence permit. As a result, all of the children were exiled with my grandfather from the city in which we lived and sent to a poor village in which schooling was limited and appallingly backward. Then came the Great Proletarian Cultural Revolution, which closed down all schools for three years and all colleges for twelve. I spent my teenage years doing manual labor—first in the countryside, and later, in an urban candy factory.

Paradoxically, this turn of events may account for how I acquired an independent mind, since I was spared the mind-numbing political education that all students were force-fed at the time in schools throughout China. Not only did I not accept the political doctrines of the time, but I actually devoured all the banned books I could put my hands on, absorbing them like a dry sponge. I secretly recorded my thoughts in small notebooks or on scraps of paper and hid them under my bed, since I had no one with whom to share them. (Later, with the aid of my parents, the authorities collected all these writings and used them as evidence against me.) The more I read, the more I was inspired to think independently, and the lonelier I became. The occasional revelations of liberty in the outside world that came through in the works of the various authors whose books I could get hold of were the only silver linings in my otherwise dark, cloudy days.

My loneliness was ultimately eased by social activism. I kept looking for like-minded people. Two months before my eighteenth birthday, I saw a poster on a public wall. The article on it demanded democracy and rule of law. It touched on forbidden issues and gave voice to my own convictions. Without considering the danger, I reached out to the authors and joined their endeavors as a political dissident. With my newfound friends, my intellectual powers could be fully engaged. We built a friendship based on shared disapproval of the prevailing ideology, and on our conviction that sacrifice would be necessary if China were ever to have a new political future. The friendships were so intense and rewarding that ending up on the wrong side of the authorities seemed a small price to pay. Actually, it didn't even feel like a price at all, since I gained a community for which, I began to realize, I had been longing my entire life.

Defiance was thus more or less built into my character, and that character more or less drove my destiny. No one who knew me well was surprised when I was taken into custody by the authorities in 1977 and locked up in solitary confinement, where I spent my twenty-first birthday.

My salad days took place against the backdrop of a tragic and tumultuous time in China. The Communist takeover, collectivization, the Great Leap Forward and the Cultural Revolution—one brutal and crazy political melodrama after another—took the lives of tens of millions of people and left no one unscathed. Persecution, public humiliation, imprisonment, and death were daily realities. From 1966 to 1978, universities stopped accepting students. The economy took a nose dive each time a political campaign was launched. Hunger, disease, and rationing were part of the daily grind. Misery was normal, and so was insanity. Even if I had wished to pursue a "normal" life, there really wasn't any such thing.

Some of my American friends have used the word "tragedy" when they hear stories of my early life. But the real tragedy is that however unique my story seems, it was actually *everybody's* story in those days. It was normal for people in my generation not to have enjoyed an innocent childhood, not to have had proper schooling, to have been sent off to do harsh, manual labor in rural areas or factories and to be persecuted in myriad ways for having "incorrect" thoughts. I have never met any Chinese person around my age who does not have some horror story to tell: a relative or a neighbor jailed or killed, or one who committed suicide; a child publicly denouncing his parents; a teacher tortured by her students; a teenager doing backbreaking labor and not having enough to eat. We grew up accustomed to fear, turmoil, poverty, and scarcity.

My story, therefore, is to a great extent also the story of my generation: China's baby boomers. In the 1980s and 1990s, they made a quantum leap from Communism to capitalism, and have since, paradoxically, become the backbone of China's recent economic miracle.

On the surface, of course, nothing about the China of 1967 remotely suggested the China of 2007. But on reflection, I think it can be argued that the seeds of the great transformation—or, to use official Chinese government terminology, the era of "economic reform and openness"—were actually planted during those years. This makes the story of my generation the story behind China's economic rise. Born and raised under the Maoist version of Communism, they understand only too well that there is a dark side of any seemingly attractive ideology. They have turned into non-believers, rejecting all big ideas—Communism, socialism, and certainly egalitarianism. Disenchanted, realistic, and anti-ideological, this generation was driven headlong by the melancholy of Maoism into the arms of the most pragmatic form of capitalism in human history. In this version, there is no room for populism, empathy, or public responsibility.

And that is precisely where my story begins to deviate from that of my contemporaries who have remained in China. In 1987, I came to the United States, and was fortunate enough to do it on a Harvard fellowship. I became part of that Chinese exodus of the 1980s in which tens of thousands of members of the not-so-young generation began to work assiduously to leave the country. Some of us ended up in America and began to pursue our own versions of the American dream. On my way to America, I dreamed about having all the books I desired to read, learning all the subjects about which I was curious, and speaking out about all I wanted to say. Also, on a less lofty level, I dreamed about "having meat whenever I want," as my kid brother used to wish; that was about the limit of our imaginations when we thought of what it would be like to be truly rich.

After I arrived in America and began to get a feel for the place, something inside of me suddenly clicked. Everything—my heart, my soul, my mind, and my personality—somehow felt at home. I felt freer than I had ever felt before, and inadequate no more. I could speak my mind and was appreciated by others at the same time, even when they didn't agree with me. I felt that all my life I had actually been an American at heart.

On March 29, 2001, I raised my right hand and was sworn in as an American citizen. The first thing I did after the ceremony was register to vote. That same evening, I attended the Radio and Television Correspondents' Dinner, an annual Washington event that attracts no lesser a light than the president of the United States. Not being much of a Bush fan, I wasn't paying much attention to the president, who was up on the stage telling jokes. But suddenly, I heard the host call my name. He congratulated me on becoming a citizen. I saw the president applauding and smiling—and it was all broadcast live on C-Span.

After the episode, someone asked me about my reaction to this whole turn of events. "I might not vote for Bush," I said, "but I will surely fight for this country."

I like to remind myself why I chose to be an American. In one sense, everyone who lives here makes this choice, or else their ancestors did. I remember once, during an academic conference, a speaker was discussing the beliefs, behavior, and voting patterns of a "typical American," by which he meant residents of white, middle-class suburbia.

"Sir, I don't think that I agree with you," I raised my hand and said. "I believe *I* am a typical American."

"How so?" He seemed amused.

"Because," I replied, "the American dream often has an accent."

Actually, I was not sure if I was a typical American. I didn't know what a typical American looked like, or if his or her look mattered at all. I only knew that I came here to escape political persecution, to achieve personal freedom, and to pursue happiness. That was, at least to me, American enough.

STORY ONE: A PHONE CALL FROM HELL

During my second semester at Harvard, my adviser called me one evening.

"Please come to my place tomorrow afternoon. We need to discuss your future." He spoke in Chinese. One of the leading Asian experts in the world, Professor Ezra Vogel was a fluent Mandarin speaker. His voice was normal, even friendly, and I detected no sign of discontent or hostility.

Still, on the receiving end, I began to tremble. What had I done wrong to result in such a phone call? Why did my adviser—who, in the social framework I brought with me from China, I reflexively considered my leader or supervisor—want to talk to me about my future? Something must be terribly wrong here.

That five-minute phone call robbed me of an entire night of sleep. As I tossed and turned, I reviewed my performance in school: like most Chinese students, I had good grades, but I also resembled them in my unwillingness to open my mouth much during seminars, for I was barely able to keep up with the discussions between professors and other students. Could that be the problem? Or was it something else? Had I said or done something that irritated someone in the department? Had the school decided to cut funding to foreign students, and was I about to lose my scholarship? Eight hours was long enough to consider a broad range of improbable causes for my misery.

Yes, misery—and one deeply rooted in my past experience. Whenever I had been ordered to discuss my future with my superiors, something was always horribly wrong, and harsh punishment inevitably followed. God alone knew how much I wished that people in authority would just leave me alone.

Take one incident as an example. In the spring of 1977, when I was working the day shift in my factory—a confection processing plant with a thousand employees—two officers from the factory's security department approached me. These were Communist Party cadres with considerable power, entirely different from the security guards you see in American office buildings. Every workplace had them, and rank-and-file employees always dreaded interactions with them.

The cadres informed me that there would be "a discussion about my future" between my superiors and me, and then immediately led me away.

The Party secretary at my factory (referred to in China as my work unit), the head of the security department, and a stranger wearing a military uniform (but without the usual military ornaments—a fashion in the 1960s and 1970s designed to show one's military connections) were sitting at one end of the office. They were all smiling, but it was a kind of "gotcha" smile, signaling unmistakable power over an object, i.e., me. They pointed to a stool and motioned for me to sit on it. The eight feet between us created a space filled with a mixture of their authority and my anxiety.

The Party secretary began the interrogation. Speaking at a deliberate pace, he asked: "What's on your mind these days? Have you been engaged in any wrong-thinking or wrongdoing? Anything you want to confess to the Party?"

Having grown up in the shadow of the Party, I was constantly prepared for such questions. Everybody was. Yet I could not hide my nervousness when I told them I could not think of anything to confess.

"You must carefully consider your future! You certainly know the Party's policy: mercy for those who confess, and severity for those who resist! You have freedom of choice: you can choose between darkness and light. The Party today is making a final effort to save you."

A "final effort to save me." I knew what that meant. During the prior two years, I had been under constant surveillance for participating in "anti-Party" activities—questioning the Communist system, criticizing the government, and sharing seditious thoughts with close friends. In the eyes of the Party, I had been engaging in the most dangerous type of subversion. "Here it comes," I thought to myself; I had seen this movie before. It was part of the procedure to humiliate the victim before crucifixion. It was less a final *effort* than a final *solution*.

Ten minutes later, these party "leaders"—the one with army uniform turned out to be the police bureau chief—informed me that I would be placed in solitary confinement for an unspecified length of time.

"We are giving you an opportunity to reflect on the crime you have committed," I was told.

I was not really surprised. I had grown up with such things. Almost all of the adults in my extended family had experienced some form of persecution or another, ranging from short confinement of a few months' duration, to a few years of hard labor in various forms of concentrations camps, to a decade-long jail sentence.

Struggling to retain my dignity, I quietly stood up, untied my apron (my work uniform), and followed the security cadres, who led me to my cell. I tried to find out the anticipated length of my detention by asking if I should tell my family to bring me some winter clothes. No one gave me an answer. That was expected, too, from numerous stories I had heard from friends, family, and neighbors who had had similar experiences.

I remembered the story of one of my relatives who had also been incarcerated. He recalled that more than a dozen times, he had been taken out to a field with other prisoners by armed guards. Noticing that some prisoners were given food, he asked for his share.

"You will wait your turn until we come back," the guard said.

Before long, he realized that those given food were the ones slated for execution, while those with empty stomachs were to survive. He began to pray for an empty stomach. The lesson was always to ask, in the hope that some information would slip through, even though you know the guards have been instructed not to provide specific information.

Refusal to specify the term was designed to be part of the punishment. They led me to think I would stay in this cell indefinitely, and to believe that the situation would keep deteriorating. The threat of indefinite punishment was powerful leverage. In my greasy, smelly work uniform, I realized my future would likely include months of confinement. My twenty-first birthday was coming up in a few months. Perhaps I would be out at twenty-two? Twenty-three? Or twenty-five? Or would I be soon transported from this informal detention cell to a large penitentiary? My aunt, an accused counterrevolutionary, had already spent eleven years in a small cell. Would that be my future as well?

Of course, I did not control my future. Rather, it was the province of people around me, especially my "leaders." Like birds of prey, they always hovered over you, flying in circles, waiting for you to make a move, and, when you did, swooping down and tearing you to pieces. Powerless as I was, there was no other choice but to wait to learn my fate. Whenever I was summoned to a conversation about my "future," I felt like a prisoner being taken, heart pounding, to face a firing squad. Learning never to shed tears in front of my persecutors, no matter what dreadful punishment was meted out, and keeping my dignity were my only forms of redemption.

So, a decade later, when I rang Professor Vogel's doorbell that afternoon, I managed to look very composed, though a little pale from a sleepless night.

Ezra did not notice. He invited me in and served me tea. Then he said, casually, and in English, "I want to discuss your future with you. What are your plans for research and a dissertation?"

This was the question about my "future" that had cost me a whole night of sleep! So why had I been anticipating misfortune? I suddenly came to the realization that my personality, my lifestyle, my view of the world, and my way of dealing with relationships had all been completely shaped by fear. Fear dominated the society in which I had grown up. Almighty fear pervasively ruled every corner of the culture in which I was brought up, dictating our thoughts, our behavior, and our lives.

We learned at a very early age how to act and react, how to conform, and how to perform, based on very specific rules. Rules that had to be obeyed, or severe consequences would surely follow.

Fear did more than that. Making people afraid was only part of the strategy. It was the beginning of the game of dictatorship in shaping a collective national personality. Threatened by constant fear, we took the same path as animals in confinement. We began to see our cell as our universe and tried to find interesting things in a narrow space to fill our empty lives. Since we were human beings, we could do even better than the animals: we could reason about our confinement, and try to make sense of it. Many—if not the majority—of us convinced ourselves that we were not really in confinement. We were, rather, soldiers in a great camp guided by historical destiny. We transformed political doctrines and political systems, imposed upon us with terror, into faith, values, and lifestyles. We even internalized them into our personalities, our psychology, and our instincts. In so doing, we were able willingly to violate common decency, applauding cruelty toward other human beings for the sake of the political institution and even taking part proudly in such actions. We turned misery into triumph—or at least into the illusion of triumph. Fear thus not only took away our freedom, but also took away our ability to reach freedom. Our souls were chained to an empty promise, a promise of the greatness of Communism.

Human history has recognized that the political system under which my countrymen once lived is coming to an end. With China's newfound capitalism and prosperity, memories of the old days are fading away quickly. Yet the fear that once penetrated our blood has left its legacy. Its ghost still dictates many aspects of our lives, and binds our souls in many ways.

I am writing to confront the ghost of the past, and to free my soul.

STORY TWO: MY FANTASY ABOUT AN ORPHANAGE

The seeds of fear are usually planted in the early years. For me, fear started with a minor incident at age six. It was so minor, in fact, that my parents totally forgot about it; yet it was so major to me that I still vividly remember all the details as well as the shadow it cast on the rest of my life.

My father's cousin married the Party secretary of a county in Guangdong Province. When the couple came to visit us, they brought me a toy—a plastic panda. It did not last very long and was soon broken. Before long, I had forgotten all about it.

One day, a peddler passed by our home, hawking maltose, a popular candy at the time. People could pay either with cash or with used plastic or rubber goods. I wanted the candy, found the broken toy, and exchanged it for a piece of candy. Since I had the impression that my toys were my own, I had no reason to anticipate any trouble, and I soon forgot the episode entirely.

It never crossed my mind that the neighborhood surveillance system might actually be watching *me*. Why would someone watch a child getting candy? But someone was watching, and the transaction was reported back to my parents.

That awful day, that dreadful afternoon, my father called me in with thunder brewing inside him. He had the kind of expression that had become far too familiar to me, a face that made me tremble like an autumn leaf. He asked about the plastic panda. Shaking, I told the first lie of my life: I said the toy had been lost.

Mother, who sat beside him, put in her two cents.

"Find it immediately. If you are lying to us, your punishment will be doubled."

I expected to be beaten, as I had been in previous incidents. Pretending to make all possible efforts, I searched everywhere: in boxes, under the bed, and in some unlikely corners. Meanwhile, I was confused. Wasn't the toy supposed to be *mine*? Why would trading it to someone else be a crime? Not that I could possibly utter any of these protestations. I was far too frightened to do that.

My efforts led me nowhere, naturally. My parents then announced that they knew I had lied. They knew what had become of the toy—I had *stolen* it. If I didn't confess within two days, they threatened, I would be sent me to the "children's reformatory," a place for juvenile delinquents. I would be locked up and treated harshly there. Worse, it would leave me with a criminal record for my entire life. As a convicted thief, I would be humiliated in front of the entire human race. No one would ever befriend me again.

Growing up a in a Communist country, I was raised as an atheist, so I never had a clear picture of what children in the West are told about hell. I'm convinced, though, that no hell could match the terrifying picture of that reformatory. The worst part of my image of it was not even the physical punishment and pain; it was constant public humiliation and eternal personal isolation. This hell was presented to me as my future—a future that would commence in just in two short days. I was too frightened even to remember that I had another choice: to tell the truth, and to be beaten as a consequence.

The two days that followed were the most horrible period in my entire life. My parents started to gather my things into a big green net, discussing in front of me all the while how they would take me to the reformatory, and ignoring me. Standing there watching them, my eyes remained dry, but tears welled up in my chest, which caused a choking pain. I trembled uncontrollably, feeling as though I would be the next thing to be thrown into that net, waiting to be shipped off to hell. Day and night, I wished for a miracle—suddenly finding a similar toy on the street, being rescued by some faceless hero, getting severely ill and being hospitalized, or even being run over by a truck. Any miracle that could save me from doomsday would be fine. For the first time in my life, I couldn't sleep through the night. My entire being felt as if it were being sucked into the hollow of the darkness. I was in pain, mentally and physically. Ever since that time, pain, hidden in my body, has a way of surfacing whenever I take a wrong turn in life.

Since I was only six years old, I did not end my life that night—perhaps because I had no idea how to do it. The day before my scheduled departure, I realized I had another alternative. I told my parents the truth. Aware that I had been punished enough, they did not beat me but did give me a long lecture. So overwhelming were my mixed feelings of relief and exhaustion that I don't think I heard a single word of it.

Later, as a teenager, I realized there was no way my parents could actually have sent me to a reformatory based on that incident. I understood that *they* had lied to *me*, too. Still, I could not help imagining from time to time that if they had actually sent me to that place, my childhood might actually have been far happier. When I was twelve, I read two books by a Soviet writer, the principal of a reputable orphanage and reformatory in Ukraine. Students there were mostly orphaned juvenile delinquents—thieves, robbers, child prostitutes, etc. The reformatory provided them with warmth, protection, and education, shielding them from the brutality of the outside world. The principal, a fatherly Ukrainian named Anton Semyonovich Makarenko, with his funny glasses and Russian, or Ukrainian, sense of humor, became my secret hero. I even wished he had been my guardian. I fantasized that I had somehow become an orphan (although I never actually imagined my parents' death) and was sent to that reformatory. All the trouble and pain in my life would come to an end. In the drizzly days in Guangzhou, the city in which I grew up, I often stood in front of our narrow window, staring at the gray sky, daydreaming of the broad, flat Ukrainian plain and the deep blue sky above it. The sun was shining, the warm wind was blowing, and a group of cheerful youngsters with cute shorts or skirts were running and laughing. I imagined being part of their laughter, their freedom, their friendship, and their love affairs. And presiding over all of us there forever was this great guardian—the gray-haired principal, the ultimate father figure.

The wound from my parents' betrayal never healed. Not really.

If their goal had been to stop me from lying to them, they failed completely. After the plastic panda incident, fear dominated my life in that household. Living with my parents, I felt imprisoned. Instead of expecting protection from them, as most kids did from their parents, I regarded mine as a source of fear and potential harm. The more they demanded my trust and obedience, the more I pulled away from them. I carefully hid my thoughts and feelings, preserving a tiny space in the corner of my mind for my imagination to run free. Yet I was never able to hide my mistakes and my wrongdoings in school from them. My parents had considerable influence at the school I attended. Teachers reported all the details of my performance to them. This surveillance kept me on constant alert. Since they would not let me go free, I certainly would not let them have me—the *complete* me. My childhood, together with its innocence, was slowly drained away in this endless confrontation with my parents.

Ironically, both of them were child psychologists. But they were trained in the early 1950s by Soviet experts, of course, for whom cruelty was the name of the game. I still don't understand why fear was so often used by adults as a tool to control children, particularly when the children trusted the adults completely. Between parents and children, the more fear there is, the less respect, trust, and love there is. Children who grow up in fear are molded by fear. Fear promotes mistrust, anxiety, and even hatred, and takes away innocence, joy, and simplicity.

In a perverse way, I benefited from learning fear at an early age. I learned to develop a kind of double personality. On the surface, I was a senseless and troublesome kid, not caring to obey social rules. Inside, however, I cultivated a colorful world of imagination and freedom. By the age of seven or eight, I became well known in my neighborhood as a bookworm. When other kids were playing outside, I usually hid in my room with my nose in a book. Neighbors noticed that when other parents urged their kids to go home and start their homework, my mother would loudly order me to put my books down and go out and play. For my part, I carefully kept my distance from my parents. The internal, imaginary me—increasingly a stranger to my parents—was effusive, honest, and funny, and had a lot of friends. Most importantly, she was happy and loved. Like a bird embryo in its shell, I was growing, but within the confines of the imaginary world I created for myself. I was waiting for the day when I would be mature enough to break the shell and take control over my own life.

In this way, my childhood slipped away.

And while the couple who gave me the plastic panda never had a clue about the misery their gift brought me, as it turned out, they had their own share of misery to deal with. In 1967, during the peak of the Cultural Revolution, the husband was persecuted. He was taken away from his family and put in solitary confinement. For a few months, he was publicly humiliated on the street and brutally beaten every day. Finally, someone put an end to his misery. His body was found at the bottom of a pond, with a large stone tied to his waist. Like those of hundreds of thousands—perhaps millions—of other murders that occurred in those years, his case was never solved, and the murderer, or murderers, was never caught or punished.

Figure 1. Our family in Guangzhou in 1960. Back row: My aunt (mother's youngest sister) and her husband (a geologist); the husband of my other aunt (a party cadre and Moscow-trained economist) and my aunt (my mother's younger sister who was in jail for eleven years). In the front are my father, me, Grand-ma, my brother James, and my mother. My sister was not in Guangzhou at the time the photo was taken, and my other brother was not yet born.

STORY THREE: GRANDMA'S GOLD MOUNTAIN

Actually, the orphanage was not my first choice of a place to live. My grandma's place was. It was my grandma who taught me about happiness, common sense, honesty, and, most important, kindness to other human beings.

I was born in Beijing in the summer of 1956. When I was four months old, my parents sent me to be raised by my grandma, who lived in Guangzhou, also known as Canton. My grandma had three daughters, of whom my mother was the eldest. Although I was her second grandchild, I was the first one she actually raised.

Grandma's home was located in the center of Guangzhou, in a three-story building with six fair-sized apartments. The entire neighborhood consisted of identical brick buildings. The flat tops of the buildings were connected; one could literally visit a whole string of them without going through another front gate. When the weather permitted, families would put their dining tables out on their porches or rooftops and invite their neighbors over for a bite of food or a game of cards. Flowers and plants adorned many roofs, reflecting a Cantonese obsession. When I grew older, I learned that all the buildings in this neighborhood had been erected by Chinese people who had made their fortunes overseas. Years later, when I had a chance to explore old neighborhoods in some of America's East Coast cities like New York and Baltimore, I recognized the style of these early twentieth-century buildings whose rooftops were used by neighborhood kids as important travel routes. Apparently, the overseas Chinese imitated the architecture in their adopted country in their own homeland. The familiar surroundings made me feel more at home.

My first memory of life in Guangzhou was of an iron fence outside our apartment. Such fences can still be found in some old buildings in the States. I often grasped the iron bars tightly; they were icy cold in winter and sizzling hot in summer. I tried, with little success, to shake the fence, and to reach the street—it was only about ten feet wide, but seemed many times that. Later on, the fence mysteriously disappeared. I learned many years later that it had been taken by the government in 1958, during the Great Leap Forward campaign, to be used as raw material for iron and steel production. Like many other household items taken during this misguided movement, it undoubtedly became a piece of useless scrap, lying somewhere in a rusty heap.

The next memory was of salty preserved fish. We had this fish at every meal, and though it was considered a great source of protein, it soon made me want to vomit. That was the so-called "three years of difficulty" period, a disaster created by Mao Zedong's Great Leap Forward campaign. At least twenty million people starved to death; possibly it was as many as forty million. Historians argue, but who can really tell? It was surely the greatest man-made famine in human history. Hunger was evident at every family dinner table, and disease was visible on everyone's faces—puffy skin resulting from drinking too much water to fill empty stomachs. People ate everything imaginable, including dead human bodies. Compared to most, I was living in heaven on earth—I had salty fish. Grandma saved as much as she could to feed me.

Grandma had many relatives in Hong Kong and overseas. In those difficult years, people in Hong Kong sent food to China to aid their relatives. Those who had such helpful relations were considered the most fortunate. It was said that the Hong Kong post office was not able to handle as many parcels as it received, and so quotas were imposed. The most common parcels thus consisted of salty fish soaked in grease or powdered milk, foods that contained a maximum amount of protein. I heard a story from one neighbor that someone he knew died from eating a whole pound of powdered milk on a very empty stomach and drinking water afterward. For years, the memory of that story kept me away from powdered milk.

Grandma must have lived alone for a long time. Before I appeared, she had acquired the habit of constantly talking to herself. At her side, I heard all kinds of stories and a lot of neighborhood gossip. One of the terms she used most often was "Gold Mountain." She gave me a detailed description of that wonderful, golden place. Grandma murmured that everyone wanted to go to Gold Mountain. If you worked hard there, you would have plenty to eat and to wear. Gold Mountain had tall buildings everywhere. It also produced the biggest and most beautiful oranges in the world. People in Gold Mountain used real gold as money. After someone earned his gold, he would put the gold inside a bamboo trunk and carry it back to China to build houses. The house we were living in was built in such fashion by my mother's grandpa, who had gone to the Gold Mountain a long time before and carried back a trunk full of gold.

Many of my childhood dreams centered on this mysterious and extraordinary place, which was one of the favorite subjects of the daily chat between Grandma and her friends, mostly other old ladies in the neighborhood. They would mention that someone came back from the Gold Mountain, someone built a house somewhere with money from the Gold Mountain, or someone from the Gold Mountain came back to China and married a nice girl.

I had no geographical sense of this Gold Mountain. Nor did I realize that neither Grandma nor any of the other *ah po* (old ladies) had ever actually seen the place. Listening to Gold Mountain chat when half asleep on my grandma's back, I constructed a most lively Gold Mountain in my vivid childhood imagination. It had tall, colorful buildings with steep roofs pointing up to the bluest sky. On the streets, everyone carried solid bamboo trunks. And golden oranges floated around everywhere, luring people to pick them up. How I wished I could be there!

I made a pledge to myself that I would go someday.

Years later, when I was in the second year of elementary school, I mentioned my dream of the Gold Mountain to a classmate. She looked at me with a strange and almost disgusted expression, and spoke to me in strong tones of condemnation:

"Gold Mountain! That's in America. You are praising the American imperialists!"

Never! I tried to argue, tried to reason with her, and tried to cling to my childhood dreams, but she would not listen. Instead, she reported me to our teacher.

The teacher did not make a big fuss about it, luckily. After all, I was only a stupid seven-year-old. However, she did confirm that my precious Gold Mountain—which I learned much later is known in English as San Francisco—was, indeed, an American city.

I was devastated. How could that beautiful dreamland, with its tall rooftops, bamboo trunks and big oranges, have anything to do with the ugly, imperialist America of government propaganda? Worse than that, how could my beloved grandma and her good-hearted friends be spreading pro-American propaganda? That in itself could easily have amounted to a counterrevolutionary crime in those days.

Confusion tortured me for years. I was unable to find an answer anywhere. Only seven years old, I had already learned to keep such questions to myself. In the midst of anti-American frenzy, even raising an issue like that would surely bring about trouble for me and my grandma.

This was only the first in a string of confusing questions that tormented me throughout my childhood and adolescence. I found myself constantly torn between things I loved on the one hand, and the contrary political teachings of the Party on the other. I was never willing to condemn the literature, music, or history that I enjoyed but that was labeled as "reactionary" and banned by the Party. Nor did I know how to draw a line between myself and those "backward" or "evil" people, and avoid eventually becoming one of them. Similarly, I never acquired the art of praising and repeating poorly written pieces of official writing, or the capability of sucking up to party personnel. As a political survivor, I was thus severely handicapped.

My father detected the problem long before it surfaced. When I was five, he came back to the city from the north and took me away from my grandma, in spite of the old woman's tears and protests. For the next twenty years, my father reminded me whenever he had the chance that I had been the victim of my grandma's politically incorrect, "pro-bourgeois" influence. He accused my grandma of poisoning my mind and limited my visits to her to once a week.

My father, of course, was not entirely wrong. Grandma was the only adult in my life who was not affected by the poisonous political atmosphere of the day; she simply did not give a damn about politics. She did not care if I was politically successful, and did not expect me to become a Party activist. She judged other humans by traditional standards and taught me to do so, too. A good person was a good person, whether or not the Party approved of him; a bad thing was a bad thing, regardless of what the Party propaganda indicated. Under her guidance and protection, I was able to be the child I wanted to be. I could cry when I was sad and laugh when I was happy. I could be myself, and she loved me for me being me. During the difficult days of my life, when I was publicly condemned as a villain, Grandma was the only one who remained faithful to me. In those years of political terror, it was she who passed on to me an appreciation for the most important aspects of our human heritage: love and kindness. She was, and still is, the Gold Mountain of my life. I cherish every minute I had with her.

Civilizations are vulnerable. It takes hundreds of generations to build one, like that of China, which has existed for five millennia. But they can be destroyed in only one or two generations. One brutal regime can kill a mature society, just as one blow can kill a human being. Without people of the older generation like my grandma, who can pass on traditional values, younger generations, born and raised under such a regime, are forever doomed.

In 1987, three months after I came to the States, Grandma passed away. Writing about her now, I realize that I had precious little knowledge about her as a person—about her feelings, her joys, her pain, and her life story. I do not know what kind of family she came from; neither do I know the story of her early years, her marriage, or her dreams. I can recall only a few fragments, but to me, even such fragments are fascinating.

What I do know is this: Grandma was born in the beginning of the twentieth century in Taishan County, Guangdong province. Taishan, also known as Toisan, and three other counties nearby, produced the majority of the Chinese who traveled abroad before the end of the Second World War. Toisanese, a Cantonese dialect, is still one of the major languages in some old Chinatowns in the States, such as those in New York and San Francisco. Almost every household in the region sent adult males to America and other parts of the world.

Grandma's father was among the Chinese coolies who came to the United States in the nineteenth century as railway workers. Perhaps because of the western influence in her hometown, Grandma never experienced foot binding, the painful practice inflicted on most young girls in her generation. She even went to school for four years, and learned how to read and write. This was unusual, too. However, even more unusual was that she separated from my grandpa, and, in the 1940s, actually divorced him.

I never heard Grandma mention my grandfather. I learned of his existence only when I was about twenty. He lived in the same city, but I never met him. Nor did I have any desire to do so. From other relatives, I learned that Grandpa's father had also gone to the United States to work as a laborer, joining the large number of Chinese immigrant workers in America during the Gold Rush years. Later, my two great-grandfathers both opened businesses—perhaps a laundry or a restaurant, or something like that. Typical Chinese immigrant stories.

My grandfather went to the States at an early age, got an American education, and became a lawyer. This was, once again, typical for second-generation American Chinese. Grandfather then went back to China and opened a law firm there—not so typical. The reason he went back, I was told, was that he loved Chinese archeology, and was especially fascinated by ancient paintings and characters—ideograms that our ancestors carved on oracle bones, stones, and bronze utensils three or four thousand years ago. While practicing law, he also established himself as one of the leading authorities on ancient characters and as an art collector.

I suspect, however, that besides archaeology, Grandfather had another passion: women. This could also have motivated him to stay in China. Anyway, while still married to my grandma, he apparently got himself a concubine. This was not atypical among rich Chinese men in those days, and was seen as no big deal—except by Grandma. Unfortunately for him, she was not a typical Chinese woman. She actually sued him for bigamy in the High Court of Canton—an action unheard of in the 1940s.

I have no idea how much Grandma understood about the law and her rights. She surely underestimated the powerful forces arrayed against women in that society, not to mention the power and connections of my grandfather, who was a prominent lawyer in the city and a rich and famous man. In any event, she lost the lawsuit, and lost her marriage as well. She became a divorcée and lived by herself for the rest of her life. This, too, was most unusual in her generation.

In all those years, I never heard Grandma complain about her marriage or her single life. Was it because the hurt was so deep that she had buried it in a corner of her heart? Or did she simply not want a man in her life? I also could not help but wonder whether she dreamed of going to the Gold Mountain herself. Did she know that she would certainly have won the lawsuit, or at least a decent settlement, had it been filed in the Gold Mountain?

I am eternally grateful to Grandma. She gave me a Gold Mountain—a place where I could let my imagination run wild, a safe haven in my heart. Time after time, as I strolled the streets of San Francisco years later, staring at the tall roofs, breathing the salty sea air, and watching the sea lions playing in the bay, I could hear Grandma's laughter. I knew she was with me.

Figure 2. Grandma in the early 1960s. She was in her mid-50s at the time.

Figure 3. With my aunt (my mother's younger sister), at age 3. It was 1959, and China was in the midst of the great famine.

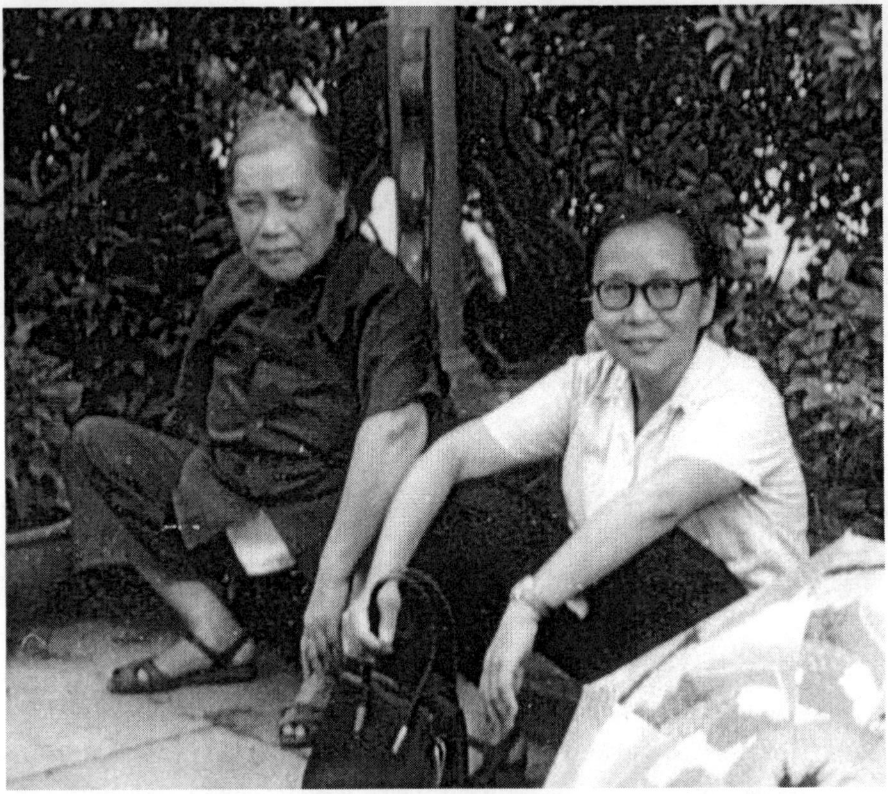

Figure 4. Grandma and Mother in the early 1980s. Grandma was a little frail. She died in 1987, three months after I left China.

Figure 5. Guangzhou's Christian cemetery. Grandma was buried next to her ex-husband, whom she had divorced many years earlier.

STORY FOUR: NO ESCAPE

My parents took me away from my grandma when I was five in order to remove me from her "politically incorrect" influence, and sent me to a kindergarten for proper socializing.

The kindergarten was established by the college in which my parents were teaching. It was located next to our apartment building. My younger brother, then three, was also enrolled there. We stayed in kindergarten for six days a week—I mean day *and* night—and were taken back home only on Sunday.

Both parents worked all the time, including most weekends. Twice a year, during the harvest seasons, they accompanied their students to an agricultural village, living and working in the fields for several weeks. Such temporary "sending-downs" were a government program aimed at "reforming and re-educating" the intellectual classes and shaping the young, urban generation through hard physical labor. Children were left in the care of the kindergarten during that period.

It should be noted that not many women remained housewives. During the Great Leap Forward campaign in 1958, the government urged all urban housewives to participate in the workforce, and so most women did. In fact, Party propaganda machine promoted campaigns that actively discriminated *against* housewives. Housewives, the government claimed, were selfish for declining to contribute to the society.

"She is a housewife," adults often whispered to their children about a neighbor, as if that were something to be ashamed of. In the apartment building in which my family lived, there were fifteen families, but only one housewife.

The educated were facing even more pressure to participate in the workforce. With only 1.3 percent of the entire population having finished a twelve-year education, anyone with a high school diploma was considered an intellectual. For educated women, therefore, not working was not even an option, unless they happen to have been fired or expelled by the government for committing political "crimes."

The main goal of the kindergarten my brother and I attended was to free parents from child care so they could concentrate on their government jobs. It consisted of only one large room and a tiny yard. A few dozen kids, aged three to seven, all lived in the same room, crowded with bunk beds. Life there was dull and rigid. The teachers, all middle-aged women, had little patience for the kids—after all, each one of them had to care for at least twenty children.

We were bound by military-like rules. Every day after lunch, for example, kids were ordered to sit on potties, whether or not they wanted to, or needed to. Collective poop time lasted for about thirty minutes, during which the teachers would take their midday naps. This would be laughable unless you were one of those hyperactive kids forced to endure the thirty-minute ordeal every day. The fabric of our lives consisted of sitting, sleeping, and playing quietly. Every day, for approximately half an hour, kids were divided into groups and were taken in turn out to the tiny backyard, where we could play with dirt and fallen leaves. Quiet kids were praised, noisy ones reprimanded. Obedience was at the core of the entire kindergarten education. We were required to develop our personalities around this central theme.

Not surprisingly, none of the kids enjoyed kindergarten, including even the most passive ones. Obedient or not, kids were kids, and they wanted to have fun. Their parents, however, seemed content with being lucky enough to have a kindergarten available to them. Most families lived within a three hundred-yard range, but few parents came to see their kids on weekdays. If a parent accidentally appeared, his or her kid would become the object of collective envy for several days. The infrequency of their visits did not mean that the parents did not care about their children. During those years, spoiling children made parents look bad, both socially and politically. It was not unheard of for a parent's work supervisor to intervene in matters related to a child's care or education, which was not in any way considered the private preserve of the parent. Since we kids did not have much to do during those long days, looking out of the windows, hoping to catch a glimpse of our parents, was our most common activity.

I was no doubt spoiled by my grandma, for she got me used to receiving attention from adults. Moreover, as a "summer monkey"—born in the summer of the year of the monkey—I was assumed to have little patience and lots of curiosity. My father found this out the first time he took me shopping, when I was about five. He plunged into a bookstore, asking me to wait outside on the street. I waited for a while, then went into the store looking for him. Unable to find him, I left the store and found a policewoman sitting behind a desk at the corner of the street. It was a lost-and-found counter, I learned later. She asked me what I had lost.

"My father," I replied.

The policewoman took down my address and led me to a bus stop. When a bus arrived, she gave my address to the bus attendant, who told me to get off the bus at the stop nearest my home. I walked home by myself, leaving my father wandering around the street in near-total panic. This incident was taken by my family forever as evidence of my lack of patience.

Anyway, I naturally hated the kindergarten. I hated being grounded. I hated being neglected. Every Saturday evening, my parents came and took me to Grandma's place, and then brought me back on Monday morning. As soon as I saw the gate of the kindergarten, I would scream, holding whatever I could find near the doorway—doorknobs, fence posts, etc., refusing to enter a place that, to me, seemed like hell. I must have been a strong kid with a strong will, because it usually took two teachers, with the help of one of my parents, to drag me in. My behavior set a bad example for the other kids, especially my younger brother. Everyone started screaming at one point or another. On Monday mornings, the kindergarten often sounded like a madhouse, with me leading the choir.

Escaping was one of my tricks that most irritated the teachers. More than once, I snuck out and went home. My parents were out at work and the door was locked, so I could do nothing but roam around the building waiting to be caught. Still, a few minutes of freedom, plus the success of temporarily escaping, gave me a real feeling of accomplishment. I have never tried drugs in my life, but I imagine it must be a similar kind of high. It was surely worth trying repeatedly, even just for the fun of it. I set a bad example, and other kids started to follow in my footsteps. At my young age, the strong desire for freedom, an instinct we inherit from our animal ancestors, easily overcame the bondage placed on us by civilization.

One day, three other kids and I noticed that the gate was open and we dashed out. One or two teachers went after us. I ran like hell, leaving the others behind to be caught. Knowing the teachers would head straight for our apartment building, I rushed into another one and hid behind the gate. I was thrilled by my achievement—free at last!

It was already late in the afternoon. Whenever I heard footsteps outside, my heart started pounding crazily.

With darkness setting in, my sense of elation gradually faded away, replaced by hunger, loneliness, and fear. What was my next move? Where could I go? Grandma's place was best, but I did not know how to get there. If I went back to my parents' place, they would certainly beat me and send me right back to the kindergarten. Apart from these, there were no other places I could even think of.

What should I do? I began to panic. At the age of five, I was facing, in a small way, the dilemma many nations face after breaking free from dictatorship. We put up a great fight to gain our freedom, but then we have no idea where to head after the battle is won. I realized that the best solution for my hunger and cold was to go back to the place from which I had escaped—the kindergarten.

It was a seminal moment for me—a lesson in the cruel reality of life. Like it or not, society doesn't change its rules to suit individual needs. Rules are rules, although they may seem ridiculous (such as our collective poop time). In fact, it is precisely because many of these rules are silly that society, or its authorities, must impose them on individuals by force. In the darkness of my successful night of escape, I began to comprehend the organization of human society and the tragedy of the grown-up world. I began to grow up myself.

In that moment of desperation, I also turned into a novelist. Based on the stories and fairy tales I knew, I constructed a story of my own. I imagined I was trembling on a street corner during a violent snowstorm. This had clearly been influenced by Hans Christian Andersen's "The Little Match Girl," a story my aunt read to me repeatedly, since, living in Guangzhou, I had never even seen snow. The next morning, my parents, who were responsible for putting me in the kindergarten in the first place, would find me—dead, of course—on the corner. They would cry and promise to send me back to my grandma. They would wrap me in warm blankets. All the other kids, including my brother, would be released from the kindergarten immediately. Everyone would cheer the heroine—me—and her triumph. I was so moved by the story I had created that I forgot about the hunger and cold and fell asleep.

The following morning, someone found me in the back of the gate asleep, and sent me back to the kindergarten. I never ran away again after this disastrous success, but I didn't become more obedient either, since obedience didn't seem to be part of my makeup. I began to think up other ways to liberate myself from the kindergarten.

One clue came from one of the other rules, the requirement that we wash our hands before meals. The teachers told us that if we did not wash, bacteria in the dirt on our hands would make us sick. What useful information! If I became sick, of course, I would be sent home! And since my parents had no time to take care of me, Grandma's home was the obvious destination.

I convinced my little brother, who hated kindergarten as well, to conduct an experiment with me. We would put dirt in our mouths while playing in the backyard. Our childhood imaginations magnified the power of dirt and bacteria thousands, perhaps millions, of times. We saw in a tiny handful of dirt a palace in which bacteria lived like kings, queens, princes, and princesses. I was scared. With my younger brother watching me, I bravely swallowed the dirt, and my brother followed. The taste was not as terrible as we expected. Afterward, we went to bed, waiting for the first impact—the attack of the bacteria.

Over the next two days, my brother and I became hypersensitive. Whenever we felt strange sensations, we would immediately think we were sick. But disappointingly, we remained healthy and active. Nothing happened to us and I was frustrated. I felt cheated. Apparently there was no escape, not really. Not for kids, and not for adults either.

STORY FIVE: BEING A DAUGHTER

I wasn't supposed to be born a girl, according to my father. He was expecting his first son, and was extremely let down by my arrival. My mother never said anything, but I guess she was disappointed as well.

My parents met in 1951, when my father was an assistant professor and an interpreter for the Russian experts at Beijing Normal University, where my mother was a young student. Father grew up in a village in Hunan Province. A very conservative agricultural region, Hunan specialized in producing stubborn men and shrewd politicians. Half of the Communist Party leadership, including Chairman Mao himself, came from the area. Mother grew up in Guangzhou, a major, modern port city, well known in the West as Canton before Shanghai even existed. Father was the only surviving child in a family of rural gentry. He received a traditional education, whereas mother was educated in a Christian missionary school operated by the American Presbyterian Church. He spoke good Russian; she spoke good English.

Somehow, fate put them together. Or, to be more precise, mother, a twenty-one-year-old student, sought out father, who, at twenty-four, was an assistant to a major Russian psychologist and a rising star in the field of psychology. He appeared to have a promising future in the early 1950s when the Soviet Union was the protector of the New China.

The Communists had taken over China in 1949, driving the American-backed Nationalists from the mainland to a small island off its east coast, Taiwan. Soon after the conflict subsided, the Communists began to reform the universities under the guidance of Soviet experts. Thousands of these Soviets—twenty thousand at their peak—had been sent to help build the New China. Their aim was to impose the Soviet model on China and change everything. They brought with them their scientific theories, their versions of history and humanity, and their entire university curriculum. All professors, especially those who had been Western-trained, were ordered to go through a new round of training. Science professors had to retake some college courses based on Soviet textbooks. Social sciences and humanities faculty were required to be trained in the Soviet version of Marxism and Leninism as the new theoretical framework for their work. Every single textbook had to be rewritten. This turned out to be a great opportunity for Father.

Like many young students in the 1940s, Father was driven into the arms of the Communists and to embrace Soviet ideals by the American-backed and very corrupt nationalist government. In 1947, his father, my grandpa, was arrested by the nationalists and condemned to execution. He had served as an officer in the nationalist army, but turned pro-Communist. At about the time of his arrest, father's younger brother, his only sibling, died of typhoid fever.

Having lost both a husband and a son, my grandma went into a deep depression and became delusional. The whole family was falling apart. Father, the twenty-year-old eldest son, bore the responsibility of carrying on the family name. The elders ordered him to get married and soon found him an appropriate girl.

The bride, whom father had never met before the wedding night, came from a neighboring village and was three years older than he.

"It's good luck to have an older wife. She will take care of the family. And three is a good number," the elders asserted. And the matter was thus settled.

On the appointed wedding night, however, father vanished. He climbed over the courtyard wall and ran into the darkness, carrying with him nothing but my grandma's gold ring.

Soon, he quietly reappeared in Wuhan, a city hundreds of miles away from his village, where the government held the annual national college admission exam. With little money in his pocket, he spent his first night in Wuhan at the famous Yellow Crane Tower, together with other homeless people. The tower was an ancient pagoda erected in 223 BC. When he woke up in the morning, his shoes were gone. Someone had removed them from his feet while he slept.

Father sat for the exam in bare feet. He achieved good scores and was admitted to Northwest University. It was in the ancient capital city of Xi'an, far north of his village, where no one from his family would be able to reach him. The university offered one of the only two Russian study programs in the country, and father went to study Russian.

Russia—the Soviet Union at the time—was the Mecca of Communism. Father dreamed about it, as did millions of idealistic young Chinese students in the 1930s and 1940s. The Soviet Union represented emancipation, enlightenment, and egalitarianism. It was the human future, a brave new world. None of them, of course, had ever heard of the Great Purge, the Ukraine famine, or the gulag.

Knowing my father and so many others like him, I can't help but wonder what they were really looking for. Was it

Communism, a grand social transformation, or simply personal liberty cloaked in an ideology? After reading so many memoirs by those young students who joined the Communists before 1949, I wondered how many of them turned to Communism to escape arranged marriages or other personal misfortunes.

Nowadays, it is absurd to link the Soviet Union with freedom in any way. History has shown that the Soviets created the most catastrophic political and economic system in human history. Yet aided by modern technology, they exercised political control so complete that little bad news leaked out. The Soviet propaganda machine delivered cultural products—literature, music, poetry, movies, etc. Wrapped in the Russian legacy—the language of Pushkin, Lermontov, Tolstoy, and Dostoevsky and the music of Rimsky-Korsakov, Tchaikovsky, and Rachmaninoff—Russian cultural products were irresistible to these young Chinese. Through them, they experienced excitement, creativity, and idealism, and imagined personal freedom and human progression. In the midst of war, bloodshed, extreme poverty, and the tight control of an authoritarian and unstable society, they tasted personal freedom in all things Russian. Even half a century of Communist disasters later, many of them, my parents included, can sing the Russian songs they memorized in their youth and recite Russian poems with intense feeling. Their eyes suddenly sparkle, and their wrinkled foreheads smooth out. Crossing time and space, they become young again.

Father studied Russian for three years. The timing was just right for him. In 1949, when the Communists took over, he was immediately offered a job in Beijing. Russian speakers were in urgent demand.

Father, who had never consummated his arranged marriage, formally divorced his bride in 1949. As far as I know, the woman never remarried. In the 1960s, I once caught a glimpse of her near father's village. She looked sixty, although she was barely forty. Her small figure and impassive face revealed little of what I imagine may have been lifelong suffering.

Although Father was educated in the modern system, his values remained quite traditional. While my parents were dating, they saw a group of children on the street one day. Father stared at the group and said to my mother, "I want that many kids!" Mother counted seven and was stunned. Father wanted mostly boys, of course. Lots of them. It was now his family obligation, especially as the only surviving son.

As was the custom, father consulted his elders on the issue of marriage. She was a good-natured girl who came from a good family, father reported about mother, but she was rather short.

Height should not be a concern, my great-aunt advised. Short women usually gave birth to lots of sons, she declared. The matter was thus settled.

Their first-born was a girl, my elder sister. A few months after her birth, mother was pregnant again. The second-born—myself—was exceptionally active, even in my mother's womb.

"It must be a boy," everybody predicted cheerfully each time I kicked.

My father's boss, a Russian, thought that I had to be a boy, too. He was given the honor of naming the first son.

"Alexander," he suggested after carefully considering a dozen others. It was a very masculine Russian name, suitable for a promising boy, he asserted. Its short version, also in Russian, was Sasha.

So, I became Sasha—*Xiaoxia* in Chinese, which means "Little Summer," to commemorate the season of my birth. And I also became a big disappointment to the family when I arrived in this world.

At first, the disappointment stemmed from the fact that I was a girl. Before long, however, I disappointed those around me further by not exhibiting the looks or behavior proper to a young girl. I was unattractive; at least that was what my father told me. And I acted like a poorly trained boy; that was what my mother told me.

"How will we marry this girl off in the future, since she is so ugly?" my father often remarked, shaking his head at my dark skin and wrinkled clothing.

My dark complexion was a legacy from my southern grandma; two of my cousins and their children inherited it as well. Sophie, my cousin's daughter, has become accustomed to receiving praise on her "beautiful tan" from everyone she meets in Florida, where she lives now. But this Cantonese trait was far less prized in China. It was considered ugly and undesirable by Chinese people at the time, who preferred the snow-white skin. I guess they still do, judging from the appearance of most of the fashion models who appear on Chinese TV. Fair skin is the preserve of women from the upper classes, who do not toil in the sun and always cover themselves up when they are outdoors. They are supposed to have light skin, and the lighter the better.

I also failed to compensate for my ugliness with virtue, as a good, homely girl was supposed to do. I wasn't quiet. I wasn't submissive. I was also uncontrollably stubborn and highly opinionated at a very young age, perhaps following the example of Grandma. On top of all these failings, I loved books and read too much. My future as a proper mate for any self-respecting man seemed grim, and Father often told me so.

Marriage meant nothing to me at that age, but I wasn't thrilled to be an ugly girl. Who would be? But I wasn't terribly bothered by it, either. Since I was taken away from Grandma's house, my mind had been at work creating an entirely different world into which I might escape. In books I found my refuge. And no matter what others said, I still loved a suntan. I was, in short, hopeless.

The 1960s were very confusing years for girls growing up in China. Traditional and Communist ideologies offered markedly different recipes for producing women considered suitable for the society. Yet the two doctrines overlapped in many areas and intermingled to form new standards. The main goal was that the Party needed to prepare women properly to become productive subjects.

Girls were trained by their families to follow tradition and be virtuous, humble, and submissive. They were required to help out around the house, while boys were given the freedom to run around, playing their war games. Girls were supposed to be cleaner than boys, and older sisters were required to take care of their younger brothers. Parents dressed their girls in vibrant colors and flowery prints, while boys wore only navy blue and white.

Schools taught girls something else. The 1960s was a time of increasingly revolutionary zeal. "The entire nation should follow the example of the People's Liberation Army," Chairman Mao declared. The military thus set the standards for school boys and girls, including fashion standards. Worn-out military uniforms became highly prized outfits among boys and girls for a few years.

The military was the role model. It was masculine. It encouraged cruelty and ferocity. It did not tolerate anything feminine, such as softness, beauty, or empathy. These "feminine" qualities were looked down upon by the overpowering and overwhelming military culture. "Male" qualities were considered superior. You could insult a boy by calling him a girl, but calling a girl a boy was considered high praise.

Of course, it was nearly impossible to suppress completely the natural pursuit of beauty on the part of at least *some* girls. A friend of mine cherished her collection of colored hair ribbons. Every morning, she would put them on before walking to school, but had to take them off prior to arrival. She did not want to be criticized by her teachers and her peers.

Girls were often torn between the more traditional approaches enforced by their families and the military-like training they received at school. Families required girls to take on more household duties than boys. Girls learned how to cook, sew, wash clothing by hand, and care for brothers. Meanwhile, schools and the government demanded that they work like boys. Whenever they were sent to work in the factories or the fields—a routine practice for students from elementary school to college in those days—girls had to work every bit as hard as boys. As a result, they often ended up working hard both around the house *and* at work.

I learned basic cooking skills when I was six, and was able to carry twice my weight—150 pounds—on my back when I was thirteen. Like many girls of my age, I was both feminine and masculine. Unfortunately, however, I was feminine and masculine in the wrong ways, because I always loved the wrong things. Mostly, I loved books. I could spend every minute reading. And I loved the wrong books, i.e., classic literature instead of Party propaganda.

"She is not only ugly. She is a bookworm! Who would want to marry a bookworm?" father often told other people. That was how I learned I wasn't marriage material.

Years later in the United States, I casually described to an American friend some of what my father had said to me. I wasn't expecting a strong reaction from her. To me, it was a small episode, and ancient history. It was almost funny.

"Unbelievable!" she said angrily. "Fathers should tell their daughters that they are beautiful, adorable and loved! Otherwise how can they expect them to be beautiful and adorable women when they grow up? Daughters need their fathers to be the first men to cherish them, so that later in life they will be able to develop good relationships with men!"

My eyes suddenly filled up with tears. A major part—a father figure who could teach me how to be a woman—had been missing from my life, I realized. Had it been stolen from me? Or had it never been there to begin with? Either way, there had been a gigantic, empty space in my heart.

By Chinese standards, father was not behaving particularly unkindly or unreasonably when he told me I was ugly. In fact, fathers and daughters were not supposed to be close. The two were supposed to give each other wide berth. After all, society—or the authorities—demanded that women be hardworking and submissive. No wonder ancient Chinese literature is nearly devoid of portrayals of father figures in the lives of young women. It was *mothers* who had the responsibility of training their daughters.

But my problem was, I could not stand my mother.

STORY SIX: MOTHER

I never trusted my mother. I doubt I ever loved her. However hard I tried, I cannot recall any kind of closeness between her and me, not even a simple embrace or a holding of hands, not to mention any heart-to-heart talks of the type that usually occurs between mother and daughter. Nothing of the kind. My mother was a stranger to me. And worse than a stranger, she was my prosecutor, my jailer and, I feared, maybe even my executioner. She was someone I worked very hard to avoid whenever possible. A thick wall existed between the two of us that no dynamite could destroy.

Not love my own mother? What a terrible thing to say! What could possibly have made this relationship go so far wrong?

When I was thirty-five, long after I was freed from my parents' control, mother once actually tried to communicate with me. On a rare occasion when I was alone with her, she suddenly turned to me and sighed, "My entire life has been such a mess!"

I felt as though I should feel sorry for her. She was, after all, my mother, and she was offering to reveal herself to me for the first time. I felt that I *ought* to want to seize the opening.

Instead, I pushed her away and spoke in an icy tone.

"Everyone is responsible for his or her own life," I intoned. "No one else should be blamed. You deal with your own mess." These were exactly the words she spoke to me—and delivered with the same cruelty—during the worst moment of my own misfortunes so long ago.

The wall still existed between us, even after all those years—a heavily guarded Berlin Wall that prevented any genuine human compassion from possible escape. It was a wall of hostility and mistrust.

Yes, mother had a miserable life. It was obvious. And like many other miserable people, she spread her misery contagiously among those close to her. My juvenile years were unbearable, in large part because of her.

What is true misery in life? I often think about this question. I have had many ups and downs in my turbulent past. I've repeatedly tasted the bitterness of pain, and swallowed the harshness of isolation and loneliness. Yet no matter how awful some of those experiences or feelings—lack of food, lack of money, hard labor, physical pain, political persecution, or discrimination of various kinds—none compare to the misery of lacking meaning in one's life, it seems to me. We human beings need to know why we are here. We need to feel that we are beings with a purpose. A meaningless life leads to depression and low self-esteem.

Based on such a standard, mother definitely had a miserable life. I don't think she ever found a real purpose, despite the fact that she was one of the smartest people I have ever known. When she was in her fifties, she could beat all her children in solving difficult puzzles. And she had four pretty smart children.

According to family legend, mother was the student with the best grades in her high school. The True Light School, founded in 1872 by Harriet Noyes, an American Presbyterian missionary, was a pioneer in women's education in China. In the 1940s, it was filled with girls from wealthy families. All of mother's siblings were educated there.

After my grandparents separated, mother, the oldest child in the family, was sent to live with my grandfather and his other wife. Although he was a man of means, Grandfather refused to give her enough money to cover the cost of the school. She ended up working miscellaneous jobs, including waiting tables in restaurants and tutoring rich girls. In a school filled with rich, spoiled young ladies, she constantly faced prejudice and bigotry because she was penniless. I imagine mother must have felt the same inadequacy as I did in my teenage years. According to my aunt, she was so depressed that she twice tried to commit suicide during that period.

At least I could imagine some connection with mother at this stage of her life. My heart ached whenever I saw people, especially young people, subjected to discrimination for whatever cause—being poor, belonging to a certain race or class, looking funny or ugly, or God knows what other reason. I could not—and still cannot—understand why some people find bullying others so amusing.

Before the age of twenty-three, I was also constantly the object of amusement of others. The trauma of discrimination tends to twist one's personality and push people toward an extreme—either extreme rebellion or extreme conformity. My mother ended up as an extreme conformist. For my part, I ended up at the other end of the spectrum—a bold and rather stubborn rebel.

Mother was obsessed with the judgment of others. She pursued compliments like a moth chases fire. Every day, she put on a show in her private and public life, playing each of the roles she had chosen. She played the good wife without much love, the good mother without much compassion, and the good party member without much belief. She acted according to scripts prepared by society. No one ever got a peek into her soul. She was a slave to her performance, a prisoner of her own ambition.

In high school, mother became a Christian. Although I lived with her for two decades, I was never able to detect any vestigial belief in Christianity in her. Instead, she kept telling us how ridiculous the stories in the Bible were, and how she teased her stupid Christian schoolmates about their faith. I suspected the reason she converted to Christianity in the first place was because it was the fashion of the time. In 1949, immediately after the Communist takeover, she joined the Communist youth league, another fashionable move.

In 1950, Mother took the college entrance examination and, according to her recollection, was one of the top winners among participants in eighteen provinces. She picked Beijing Normal University, a prestigious school that provided stipends to all its students.

The first half of the 1950s was the so-called "golden era" of China's pro-Communist intellectuals, particularly the young and the educated. The new regime brought about idealism and new faith. It mobilized an entire nation to build a new society, one ostensibly based on egalitarianism. It also successfully resisted pressure from the West, which consisted of the nations once considered superior to the entire developing world. A string of political campaigns was launched to mobilize the nation to reach the goals set by the Party and to persecute those who were its designated targets. The Party called for the young intellectuals, especially energetic college students, to serve as its warriors. For a while, this was very exciting.

Mother must have been one of the most enthusiastic collaborators in her school. The Party soon recruited her as a member, an honor granted to only a handful of students. Before long, she was assigned the job of assistant to the university's Party committee, and became a small part of the Communist machine that devoured millions of human lives.

Recalling her past glory was what made mother the happiest. She could brag endlessly about the revolutionary events in which she participated, most involving persecution of certain kinds of people such as landlords, rightists and "bourgeois intellectuals." I have no idea what kind of student she was, but one story she often told remains branded on my mind. In 1953, mother proudly proclaimed, she had led her classmates in an attack on one of her professors in the Department of Education who had graduated from a university in the States. This professor had brought a large model of a human ear into class. He took it apart to reveal the structure of the inner ear, but failed to reassemble it. The professor was thus given the nickname "Big Ear" by the students. Mother accused the American-educated "so-called specialist" of having neither knowledge nor character. Perhaps she was overcompensating for her missionary school background—at someone else's expense, of course.

Mother was an activist in the 1957 anti-rightist campaign, during which millions of intellectuals were accused of being rightists and deprived of their jobs. Many were jailed. She took special pride in her participation in one event—a struggle session against the famous rightist Lin Xiling, a twenty-two-year-old female college student who had had the temerity to criticize the Communist Party. Lin was accused of being a rightist and was humiliated on many public stages. During one such session, mother was chosen by the Party to sit on the stage and take notes in front of thousands of college students and teachers.

I did not even need to close my eyes to imagine mother—young, pretty, smart, and full of revolutionary zeal—looking down upon the target, a girl a few years younger than she. Sitting on the side of power in the eyes of the public, she must surely have felt on top of the world. Those "golden years," I suspect, associated as they were with intolerance, persecution, and destruction of human rights, must have done much to shape mother's later life. They were the years during which the Communist Party began, systematically, to silence all dissenting voices.

Mother's finest moment turned into my torment. Whenever she detected any rebellious tendency on my part, she would issue a warning to me, using Lin as a negative example:

"You think you are so smart that you can say whatever you please. But look at Lin Xiling. She was far smarter than you, and look at how she ended up!"

This episode in historical education had an unexpected epilogue. In February 1979, when I was fresh out of detention for having publicly criticized the Party, I met a middle-aged woman at a friend's home. We chatted about the anti-rightist campaign of 1957. Given my age, she was amazed at my detailed knowledge of the campaign in Beijing. Suddenly, she turned to me and asked, "Have you ever heard the name Lin Xiling?" Apparently, she was not expecting a yes answer. After all, I was only a year old in 1957. That name had not been mentioned in China in the past twenty-two years.

"Of course," I replied. "My mother was the designated note-taker during Beijing Normal University's struggle session against her. She has actually become my role model for her intelligence and courage."

That woman, with whom I instantly clicked, was, of course, none other than the infamous Lin Xiling. In 1958, by a direct order from Chairman Mao, she was sent to jail for fifteen years. Lin visited me in Beijing in the winter of 1979 after I was admitted to Peking University. We walked on a trail next to frozen Weiming Lake, on which she hadn't set foot for twenty-two years.

"I used to be very good at figure skating," she said in a dreamy voice. "The boys used to applaud me all the time." She put on a pair of skates and was ready to try again. Within her first five seconds on the ice, however, she fell down. Tears trailed down her wrinkled face. Twenty-two years of her life had been stolen from her, along with her love, her health, and, perhaps, some of her sanity. My heart ached for her, and I welled up with tears myself. I turned away to give her a moment of serenity. We never mentioned skating again after that.

I could not stand the fact that my own mother never repented her role in that gigantic robbery. She was, rather, a willing and active participant. Yet even that did not spare her from victimization in her own right.

By the time I began to know mother, that glorious period in her life had long passed. The 1957 anti-rightist campaign trapped many pro-Communist intellectuals. According to the

Chinese government's own data, 550,000 educated people were labeled as rightists, but researchers suggest that that is a very conservative estimate. Politically correct as usual, mother did not have much trouble during that movement, but father lost his Youth League membership for speaking out. It was mother's father, my grandfather, who suffered the worst impact.

I had been told by mother that Grandpa left China in the late 1940s, but came back from the United States in 1953. China looked promising in those years. Many overseas Chinese, unhappy in their host countries or enthusiastic at the opportunity to participate in the building of the New China, came back from the States, Europe, Southeast Asia, and other countries. My grandpa was one of them. He soon tasted harsh political reality, however. In the same year he returned, he was accused of being an "American culture agent." No one understood what the term actually meant, but an allegation was an allegation. It stigmatized a person. When the anti-rightist campaign began, Grandpa tried not to utter a word. Unfortunately, however, when the Party determined to target you, there was no real way out, and keeping your mouth shut offered little protection. He was asked a direct question by the representative of the Party:

"Please give your opinion of our country."

"Why ask me?" this former lawyer responded, ever mindful of good courtroom practice. "The three-volume *Selected Works of Chairman Mao* has covered every inch of the ground of our country. It is superfluous for me to say anything."

He was thus labeled an extreme rightist, and the written allegation read, "His hatred of the Party is carved in his bones, so he kept his mouth shut."

Yes, this is a literal translation. Grandpa was in and out of jail and labor camps for the next twenty years.

For no reason other than having a father and a husband in trouble, mother, the loyal activist, lost her job with the Party committee, and was given another one as a librarian—a serious demotion at the time.

Meanwhile, father felt ashamed for getting into political trouble. Through his Soviet connections, he quickly found himself a new teaching position in the remote Northeast city of Harbin. Although the act of moving out of the capital city may have seemed stupid at the time, it might actually have saved him from a lot more trouble—even from total destruction of his future. The worst days of the anti-rightist campaign had yet to come, and Beijing was the eye of the storm.

So my parents moved to another city in the turbulent year of 1957, leaving both their glory and their humiliation behind. As a Cantonese, Mother suffered tremendously in the Siberian-like cold weather. A few years later, she moved back to her home city, Guangzhou, with my father. They both taught for a while in a small college.

The honeymoon between the Soviets and China was coming to an end by the late 1950s, after Nikita Khrushchev denounced Stalin and his Great Purge. A storm of rebellion against Soviet rule swept through Eastern Europe. This worried Mao and the Chinese Communist Party. The Party began to run editorials in the *People's Daily* in 1963 publicizing its dispute with the Soviet Union. The Party argued that the Soviets under Khrushchev had turned into "revisionists" by abandoning "class struggle," and by suggesting "peaceful coexistence" with the West. The debate quickly heated up, and the Soviet Union soon became as hated an enemy as the United States—if not more so. Those who had ties to the Soviets had to watch out.

For that reason, in 1963, after the Sino-Soviet rift, my parents' fate took another unexpected turn. It was said that some top leader in Beijing had announced that psychology, which was my parents' profession, was nothing more than "pseudoscience promoted by the Soviet revisionists and the capitalists." Most psychology departments in the nation were dissolved immediately, and my parents lost both their profession and their positions in the college. They were, instead, given English teaching positions in middle schools, representing a serious loss of social status.

I always wonder what such a string of blows and humiliations did to mother. I had no idea whether she secretly blamed the Party for bringing on all that misery. One thing was for sure: her determination to be an "activist"—a loyal Party adherent—remained strong; it may even have strengthened. She continued to report all the details of her personal life to the Party leaders in her work unit, that is, her school, as if that could bring back whatever glory she had enjoyed before.

Her children were not spared in this constant reporting. Living with her, I felt as if I were leashed, day and night. She placed my daily activities under a microscope. Whenever she felt something was politically incorrect, she would tighten the leash, either by disciplining me or by reporting me to the authorities. At various points, that meant either teachers in my school or Party leaders in my work unit. The frequency of such reports sometimes astonished even those leaders, whose job description consisted mainly of requiring and acting on reports from their subordinates regarding other people.

Mother extended the police state to our home. My every move was monitored. She kept reminding me in various ways that I was ugly and unwanted. Under her strict control, I never had any nice clothes, since that was considered out of sync with a "proletarian" lifestyle.. In my early teens, I had only one pair of shoes: a pair of cheap, military-style sneakers for use during summer *and* winter. I joined the work force when I was sixteen, and continued to wear my only pair of shoes. A year later, I decided to buy myself a new pair. That week, my fellow workers and I had to do overtime—sixteen-hour work days for an entire week. After that ordeal, we all got some overtime pay, approximately ten yuan, which to me seemed a small fortune in those days. My fellow workers, several of whom took pity on me because of my shabby clothing, dragged me to a shoe store and forced me to purchase a pair of proper leather shoes.

The next day, as soon as I stepped into the workshop, the forewoman asked me to come and see her. She was apparently amazed by what had happened. My mother had already come to see her, demanding that she investigate the person, or persons, who had "lured" me into pursuing "the bourgeois lifestyle," as evidenced by my purchase of a pair of relatively expensive shoes. The forewoman, who had, in fact, been a member of the shopping gang, used all her powers of persuasion to convince mother that most workers, particularly the young girls, had leather shoes. No doubt thanks to her, mother did not punish me for this purchase.

Reporting about other people's activities to the authorities seemed to have become second nature to my mother. Whatever

I did often ended up on the desk of my supervisor. Worse than that, her surveillance extended to all of my friends. She took notes on who I went out with, who I was fond of, and what kind of people they were, and turned her notes over to the authorities. Mother accused me of having become a "backward element" because I had all these "backward" friends. They were backward, she concluded, because their families did not give them enough "political education." She felt she was doing them a favor. If she revealed who they were to the authorities, they would be able to adopt proper means to educate them. Eventually, she managed to deprive me of my freedom even to make friends. Hanging around with me simply wasn't worth the trouble if it meant they would be reported on just for doing it.

Mother was the front line of the state in the most private sphere of my life. She was the primary person from whom I had to protect myself. Better not to reveal anything to her; better not to give her any idea what I was thinking. Better not to make her aware of whom I was socializing with; better not to let her detect my weak points. Better not to have her around at all. To me, mother was more than the extension of the power of the state; she was the incarnation of the most pervasive surveillance system in human history, and she personified the totalitarian regime.

For a long time, I was not able to face the true nature of my relationship with my mother. I could not stand her, yet I could not admit, even to myself, that I disliked and even hated her. According to my cultural heritage, a mother is considered the center of family life. In classic Chinese literature there are plenty of lousy fathers, but rarely do you find a bad mother. Chinese mothers were famous for being unselfish and for making unimaginable sacrifices for their families, especially for their children. I could not help wondering what was wrong with me. Like many kids in similar situations, I was convinced that my parents must have adopted me from somewhere else. How else to explain the lack of natural closeness between mother and daughter?

Years later, I started to communicate with others who had had similar problems with their mothers. I was shocked when I found out that I was not alone in the Chinese community, particularly in my generation. Many of us had had terrible mothers, and mine may not have been the worst. I read the story of Lin Liheng, whose father Lin Biao was China's defense minister, and, at one point, Mao's designated successor. Her mother, Ye Qun, also a high-ranking state official, put her under constant surveillance and disrupted her love affairs repeatedly, resulting in two suicide attempts on her part.

But who are these mothers? Are they products of traditional culture, or of the Communist regime? I wondered, and undertook a little research project. After a series of interviews, I began to discern a common pattern among them. They generally came from families that had been well-to-do before the Communist takeover. In their school years, they were smart and fashionable, attracting great attention from their peers. When Communism became the new fashion of the 1940s, they readily converted to it, proud of being modern women.

Unfortunately, their identity as modern women was only skin deep. They were actually caught between tradition and modernity. One the one hand, as traditional women were supposed to do, they deferred blindly to the authorities, namely the Party. On the other hand, as "modern" educated women, who were supposed to be liberated from their traditional family-oriented roles, they were incapable of devoting themselves to their families. Loyalty to the Party was their only path to the fulfillment of their dream of being modern women. Shaping their children to meet the Party's requirements in the harshest possible ways was the only way they knew to be good mothers.

STORY SEVEN: SKEPTICISM

Since I had become the most unwanted kid in the kindergarten, my parents decided to send me to elementary school when I was six, a year ahead of most kids.

The school to which they took me was the elementary school attached to their college. It was one of those prestigious "experimental" schools that had been established around the country. In such schools, elementary education took only five, instead of six, years, and the curriculum was far more intense than that of normal schools. Many kids failed in the first two years and were transferred back to the mainstream schools. Experimental schools were supposed to admit only smart kids. And they rarely admitted kids under seven.

My parents were well acquainted with the principal, a lady in her late thirties or early forties. They were friends. In order to make a special case for me, the principal took personal charge of my admission test. After a few questions about my age and name, she asked, "Do you obey your parents?"

"Certainly not!" I replied, with my quick tongue.

She seemed to be in shock. I gave her an answer she had probably never heard from a child before.

"Whom *do* you obey?"

"Chairman Mao," I answered clearly and loudly.

Thinking back, I have no idea why I gave that answer. Perhaps I was annoyed at my parents' decision to choose school over Grandma's place. I refused to recognize their authority, and had to show my defiance in some way. As it happened, my impressive answer, which was unequivocally politically correct, landed me an offer of admission. I became the youngest student in the school.

School, however, unfortunately made me feel more inadequate than ever.

It was 1962, the year following the three-year famine. Food, or shortage of food, was still the central concern in every family's daily life. Mother had just given birth to my youngest brother. We had raised a few rabbits in the shared hallway of our tiny apartment. At a certain point, they would add some protein to our dining table. Harvesting grass for the rabbits was among my chores. Unfortunately, I had developed a special affection toward rabbits as a youngster while listening to my aunt read to us from *Grimm's Fairy Tales*. Raising those gentle animals and watching them be killed and eaten was thus an especially unpleasant experience for me. But the desire for food during those hungry days overrode human sentimentality. In the process of raising and eating rabbits, I had to mortify my sensitivity toward those poor animals. They were not the same species as Grimm's rabbits, I told myself.

The school presented us with rosy pictures of a society entirely different from that of our daily experience. The first lesson in our literature textbook was a poem:

My grandpa went begging when he was seven,

My father fled home to avoid famine when he was seven.

Now I am seven,

My commune has sent me to school.

Although most people knew that the commune system, introduced to the rural areas by Mao in 1958, was largely responsible for the most devastating famine in human history, few dared even to think of criticizing Mao for it. By the government's own admission in the 1980s, at least twenty million people starved to death during that three-year period. As kids, however, we were told that our nation, under the enlightened rule of the Communist Party, was the most prosperous in the world. Since we had no frame of reference to indicate otherwise, we accepted this as the truth.

The problem was that even we kids had reference points. We knew we were constantly hungry. None of us remembered ever having enough to eat. My little five-year-old brother often asked our parents, "Will I have all the pork I want to eat when we achieve Communism?"

A large dish of pork, well cooked in soy sauce, with a thick, greasy sauce filling a large bowl—that was the limit of our imagination of wealth and affluence.

How my kid brother and I dreamed of having enough to eat! Our stomachs always seemed empty. We were sure we could devour a whole pig in no time. We couldn't wait for such a bright future. Yet, the adults whispered among themselves, in the golden years, food had not been rationed. Meat had often been available on dinner tables. Tea, sugar, and candy were not luxuries. Suddenly, their bony faces appeared flushed, and their eyes narrowed dreamily. (Later I figured out that they were talking either about the early 1930s, when China enjoyed a short peaceful period, or the early 1950s, before the campaign of collectivization began to take land away from peasants.)

Those golden days were surely before my time. Naturally, I tried to find out more.

"Did people have more to eat before I was born?"

Each time, however, my question was met with a harsh response.

"The Soviet revisionists have caused some difficulties in our country. We are getting better!" Mother always followed the Party line, even at the most private moments.

Father's answer was equally rigid, but much simpler:

"Shut up, you stupid child!"

Fear then replaced the momentary gleam on their faces.

Gradually, I learned that any question bearing a hint of dissatisfaction with the Party or the society was taboo. Even raising such a question was inviting trouble, regardless of whatever supporting facts were in front of everyone's eyes.

Thinking back to my early education, I have come to the conclusion that the secret of the success of political propaganda does not lie in covering up reality and deceiving people. Facts, especially tragedies that have a great impact on vast numbers of people such as famine at the national level, are not so easily concealed. Nor are people easily deceived; even a six-year-old like me would question whether a person could live for ten thousand years. The secret of successful propaganda, rather, is to separate "facts" from "truth."

In the Chinese political dictionary, "truth" indicated correctness. A "fact," on the other hand, if it did not fit into the Party line, was not considered "correct," and would not be called "truth." People could gather facts based on common sense and daily life experiences; but only those presented in the Party line were deemed "truth." The party claimed that such "truth" was an aggregation of facts that formed a bigger picture. It was not until much later that I learned that this is the most basic method of mind control.

For example, if you experienced an extreme shortage of food and saw people starving to death, you could not call such facts "truth." The party would tell you that what you experienced was only something minor and temporary, or at most, a fraction of the whole truth. Looking at the bigger picture, the entire nation was in the best shape in its history, for it was successfully resisting the encirclement of the entire capitalist world and was being led by the Party to a bright, promised land. Human suffering was merely a price to pay for ultimate greatness.

All these ideas were very confusing, especially to a six-year-old, but soon people learned to avoid trouble simply by following the Party line. They convinced themselves that since they did not know the big picture as well as the Party, it was better to ask as few questions as possible. Clearly, common sense was the biggest enemy of dictatorship. If people merely believed their eyes and ears, the "truth" constructed by the Party would crumble. But few dared. For behind all "truth" lay an underlining theme, namely fear.

As a six-year-old, I had just begun to appreciate this adult world. School excited me. Every morning, I walked twenty minutes to school. The smell on the street, together with the wonderful feeling of freedom from kindergarten, made me smile, like any joyful child elsewhere in the world.

The excitement passed quickly, however. Not long after I began my formal education, I realized that it wasn't just kindergarten that was dull. Many activities in elementary school were tedious and boring as well.

The first thing I was not able to understand was required posture. We had six classes a day, each one lasting forty-five minutes. During that time, students had to sit up straight, with both hands crossed on top of the desk. If one moved, consciously or unconsciously, he or she would be subjected to harsh criticism and even disciplined. Punishments ranged from cleaning the classroom after class or standing in the corner to being humiliated in front of the entire class.

I was never able to remain in that position for more than ten minutes. Worse than that, I simply could not understand why it was required, and argued about it many times with my teachers. In fact, when I was concentrating on the subject matter of the class, I moved unconsciously and constantly. My face would be expressive, my body would move, and my hands would involuntarily leave the desk.

While I was deeply drawn into the lectures, my teachers were nonetheless greatly disturbed. They interrupted their classes and tried to correct me. When I concentrated on my posture, I missed the subject matter entirely. So despite being an eager learner, I broke the rules more or less continuously, and became a frequent object of school discipline.

I tried to argue with my teachers. I tried to persuade them I was absorbing everything they said, and I had my excellent grades as proof. They were not moved, however. And they were so annoyed at me for arguing with them that they punished me even more severely, which, in turn, provoked more defiance on my part.

Another argument I had with the teachers concerned their requirement that all homework be neat. Usually I had no problem finishing my homework, but I found it challenging to keep the paper clean. I complained to the teachers that if they wanted my homework clean, I would have to copy it by hand onto another piece of paper, which would be a waste of both time and paper. I made little headway, however, and usually got marked off for handing in messy work.

As in the kindergarten, I soon earned a reputation among the teachers as one of the most uncontrollable students in my elementary school. Unlike other troublemakers, I rarely engaged in fighting and never destroyed school property. Those students would usually acknowledge their crimes, apologize, and be pardoned. I, on the other hand, confirmed in my very simple and unshakable logic, usually had no clue what I had done wrong. My efforts to clear up confusion were what usually started most of my arguments with the teachers. To make things worse, I often refused to apologize, but continued defending myself out of an urgent desire to communicate and reason with others. To follow orders without understanding the reasons behind them seem to be beyond my ability.

Unable to control me, the teachers generally reported me to my parents, who, in turn, were constantly ashamed of having such a disappointment of a daughter. They usually ordered me to apologize, something I resisted in my bullheadedness. Apology was an art I never learned well.

There is no Chinese equivalent of crossing one's fingers behind one's back while telling a lie. So, when pushed hard by my parents, I would go to the teachers and say: "My mom said I should apologize to you! She said that I was wrong."

The teachers usually accepted this as an apology, while I could tell myself that it was not.

STORY EIGHT: RESISTING A NAP

All my political troubles began with a small incident in 1963: resisting taking a nap.

Before that incident, I was a troublesome kid; after it, I became a dissident. In the eyes of the authorities, I became someone who challenged their logic, questioned their motives, and looked for alternatives.

Father was the foremost authoritarian figure in our family. He never hesitated to use his fists against his children. I was beaten once or twice a week. This was common practice among nearly all the parents in our neighborhood, who consisted of mostly college professors and high school teachers. Children would tease each other after they were beaten, not because they were cruel, but because teasing actually eased the pain a bit.

"We heard your father beat you again this morning. Ha, ha!" a group of kids would say to the unfortunate victim.

"Actually, I escaped! I climbed a tree and climbed so high he couldn't reach me. I stayed there for an hour until he had to leave for work," the target would proudly pronounce.

We all knew that trick. In fact, my kid brother developed a better one. We had two bunk beds in our tiny apartment for the children. My kid brother would climb up to the top bunk of one of the beds and then jump over onto the other bed whenever father tried to hit him with his fist or a stick. The small kid was so nimble that the moment father figured out where he was, he had already changed position.

Since child beating was the norm, I never questioned it until the second grade, when I learned to read newspapers. One day,

I found my father's name in a paper. A child psychologist, he had published an article entitled "Do not beat your children."

I was stunned. Father, with his short temper, was among the most frequent offenders. Article in hand, I went to question him.

"Wicked kids must still be beaten!" he declared, impatiently.

"But you said in your article that children should NEVER be beaten!" I protested.

"You are an exception!" he replied angrily.

I could not reason with him, but I never again believed he had the right to beat us. Each time I would protest, but I would not beg for mercy. I felt that to do so would cast me in the role of the victim all over again. It might not have left any physical damage on my skin, but it would have wounded my pride and left an emotional scar, which would run a lot deeper.

One of our neighbors found a creative way to punish one of her unruly children. One day, he broke a bottle of soy sauce. The mother summoned her son and ordered him to kneel down, which he did.

"Slap yourself on the face!"

I could see this scene clearly from my hallway through their window. Tears dropped from the son's eyes. He was two years younger than I was. He slowly raised his hand and slapped himself.

"The other side! Harder!" the mother demanded.

He did as he was told, and then started howling. Then his mother let him go.

Thank God my parents never tried such a punishment on me. I would rather have killed myself than slap my own face in public. It would be much too humiliating.

In 1963, a directive from above arrived at all elementary schools. Schools should encourage students to take naps after lunch, the order said. It was supposed to be good for young bodies. Schools, in turn, requested parents to report whether their children followed the new rule. It even became a part of the schools' report cards.

An energetic child, I was never fond of sleeping. Beginning in my late teens, I only needed four to five hours of sleep a day. Disregarding the rule, I always spent nap time reading. My favorite subject was science.

My parents were very angry with me, again for a reason I could not comprehend. They started looking for new ways to discipline me.

In those days, China produced about five new movies each year. Except for fewer than half a dozen old Soviet movies, all foreign films were banned. Television was unheard of. Therefore, the showing of a new movie was like a national celebration. Schools might close, and the streets might empty out.

On the day of a new show, my parents announced that if I failed to take a nap once again, I would not be allowed to see the new movie with the other kids. Merely lying in bed would not count, they said. I must really fall asleep.

I jumped into bed immediately after lunch because I really wanted to see the movie. Moreover, if I was barred from going to the theater, I would become the laughingstock of my class. I would really be ashamed.

Even today, I envy people who can fall asleep anytime and anywhere. Once I had a colleague in my factory who was able to sleep while sitting upright through the daily political study sessions. It was a godsend.

As God is my witness, I made every effort humanly possible to fall asleep that day. I covered my head, but my mind became very active in the darkness. I counted from one to one thousand, but my mind was more full of thoughts than ever. I changed positions again and again, but to no avail.

While this was all going on, Mother got up and checked on me. I stayed still and held my breath, hoping to pass the test. Perhaps my body was too stiff. Or perhaps I looked too unnatural. Somehow, I could not fool mother. She warned that if I failed to obey the rule in the next ten minutes, there would be no movie.

The next hour was hell. I dared not move an inch or open my eyes. I kept dead still. My arms and legs felt numb and my neck ached, but I did not move.

Mother came to check a few more times. She knew me so well that my fake sleep did not fool her. At two o'clock in the afternoon, it was time to get up and leave. My parents announced that since I had failed to obey, they would go without me, leaving me alone at home. The entire neighborhood gradually emptied out.

I was totally defeated. As I watched other kids and their parents going to the theater, I would have cried had I not learned in my earlier years how useless that would have been. I thought of begging other adults to take me, but my pride prevented that. No one came to my rescue. Finally, I walked the two miles to the theater. The front gate was closed and everyone was inside. After waiting there for about ten minutes, I went back home in disappointment and shame.

In the next few lonely hours, my eight-year-old mind started to process the entire experience. What I came up with shook the entire belief system imposed on me by the society.

My parents and teachers often disciplined me for not following rules. However, for the first time in my life, I was 100 percent sure that the punishment did *not* fit the crime. I might not like the nap rule, but I did all I could to follow it. No one was affected; nothing was broken. All I wanted was to be left alone during the designated nap time, to do nothing else but read. My parents' decision was utterly unfair and an abject abuse of power. I felt that in a very real sense, after this incident, my parents lost their moral authority over me.

Decades later, when I hear expressions common in America like "this is fair" or "it is so unfair," I often recall this early episode in my life. Fairness was a concept alien to those who grew up in Maoist China and perhaps in other similar places. In fact, *unfairness* was a fact of life to which people had no choice but to accommodate themselves. Anyone who had authority, of whatever kind, insisted that he or she was entitled to be arbitrary. After all, that was what authoritarian power meant.

A powerless eight-year-old demanded fairness and did not get it. And in the process, a rebel was born.

Decades later, I still resist taking naps, even when there are no orders from above.

Figure 6. With one of my cousins. I was nine years old and had just learned how to ride that bicycle. The photo was taken in downtown Guangzhou, two blocks from my grandma's house. A few months after this picture was taken, I was sent to live in Hunan, effectively ending my elementary school education.

STORY NINE: THE FALLEN HERO

In the first half of the 1960s, the Communist Party nurtured a wartime atmosphere. "The nationalist reactionaries in Taiwan are coming to try to restore their power!" proclaimed the government. The upcoming war, real or imagined, overtook famine, terror, and all other miseries, and was made the center of national attention. The warlike mood legitimized the means for the Party to mobilize people militarily and to control the society. In the two provinces closest to Taiwan, Guangdong and Fujian, the government began to deport selected urban residents to inland cities or rural areas.

Few people volunteered. Under Communist rule, the rural areas were desperately poor. Peasants, traditionally the backbone of Chinese society, were pushed to the bottom of the social and economic ladder. As in the Soviet Union, the Chinese Communists diverted all possible resources into military and heavy industries. The atom bomb trumped the rice bowl. Resources were diverted to gun manufacturers at the expense of the farmers. Eighty percent of the population—the peasants—was made to pay most of the price.

Residents of Guangzhou, one of the most modern cities in China and one with large-scale industrial enterprises, enjoyed a much higher standard of living than those in smaller inland cities, not to mention peasants in the rural areas. Being sent out was thus seen as being "sent down." It was literally true. Being "sent down" was used as a convenient punishment for anyone targeted by the Party.

During the "sent down" campaign in 1965, the government needed volunteers for cosmetic reasons. My parents, both party activists at the time, volunteered me, the only child then living with them in Guangzhou. My other three siblings were being raised by my father's parents in Changsha, the capital of Hunan Province four hundred miles to the north. I had stayed in Guangzhou mainly because my maternal grandma wanted me to. But she could not prevent me from being "sent down" to live with my father's parents in Changsha.

Only nine years old, I had no idea how important this decision would be. I thought I was going out for something like a summer vacation, which I did take once in Hunan. Grandma was in tears when I said farewell to her, but I did not entirely understand why.

My paternal grandparents spoke a dialect I had a hard time understanding, but they treated all their grandchildren well. Before I had time to adjust to the new environment, however, a tragedy occurred. Grandpa was accused of being a counterrevolutionary by the Party and lost his job and his urban residence permit. Two months after I came to stay in Changsha, my grandparents, together with their four grandchildren, were "sent down" to live in Grandpa's home village, which he had left forty years before.

Grandpa was a tall and handsome man. Six feet tall and 155 pounds, he always kept a military demeanor. He was something of a local legend, but I only heard bits and pieces of his background from him, since he was a rather quiet person.

It was not until three years later, after he was arrested and my parents tried to appeal his case during the Cultural Revolution,, that I got a more complete picture of him, and that was because my sister and I were given the duty of hand-copying some letters to be sent out to the authorities.

Grandpa had been born into a peasant family in Hunan at the turn of the twentieth century. This southern agricultural province, with its strong extended family system, produced a disproportionate number of political, military, and cultural leaders, government officials, and rebels alike. Fully half of the original Communist leadership was from Hunan, Mao Zedong included.

The Gong family was of ancient aristocratic origin and could be traced back to the eleventh century B.C. According to the chronicle housed in the family temple in our village, the ancestor of this particular branch settled in Hunan in the late fourteenth century, after rebels drove out the Mongols and a bloody civil war wiped out almost the entire population of central Hunan. The Ming Dynasty was founded after that war, and the new emperor ordered people from Jiangxi, a neighboring province, to migrate to this area. My ancestor was among them.

The lineage grew quite large in six hundred years. It was sustained mostly by education—the family owned collective property, which paid for schools that were available to all young male members, even boys from the poor branches. Anyone who could pass the imperial exam would become the pride of the entire family, and had the responsibility of taking care of collateral relatives. I did not know if Grandpa's branch of the family had money, but he had surely received a solid, classical Chinese education.

It is worth mentioning here that until the Communist takeover, education had been at the undisputed core of the Chinese value system. The imperial examinations selected educated people for public service, and formed an entire bureaucracy based on intellectual accomplishment and merit. Sending boys to school was an obsession of every family. Those lucky enough to move up in the system were considered to have brought honor to the extended family. Of course, women were excluded in the old system, but women could still be honored if they found a way to establish themselves. Fifteen years ago, I was surprised to find out that my name had been put on public display in my county, with the title of Harvard PhD attached to it, although I was at the time still years away from actually getting my degree.

Grandpa had been very prepared to follow the ancient path to prominence, but a revolution overthrew the Qing Dynasty in 1911, and the entire nation went into turmoil. Local warlords, as well as various factions of revolutionaries, organized their own armies. Many young intellectuals abandoned Confucianism—the age-old system of relationships and behavior that had kept social order in China—and joined the military to search for new ways to save and modernize the nation, and to save their families as well. Grandpa entered the Wuhan Military Academy with five other young people from neighboring villages.

In that time of chaos and near anarchy, these young men protected their families with their uniforms. Since government barely existed, the country was effectively ruled by the ruthless warlords and bandits. Only military uniforms, which represented modern fire power, were respected. Every summer, these young men, in their new, starched outfits, would visit their families. They took turns playing "officer" in their own households, followed by five "guards"—all in a charade designed to scare off the petty thieves and bandits.

Grandpa graduated in 1926 and became a captain. He met many Communist leaders, but eventually chose to side with the Nationalists. When the Japanese invaded China in 1937, he fought hard against them.

"Waving my sword and pointing at the devils ..." Grandpa sometimes hummed as an old man. It was an old, anti-Japanese military song from the 1930s. Occasionally, he would describe some of the brutal battles to us. He recalled the battle to defend Changsha. For three days and three nights, his troops had had no break. Both sides had used dead bodies to deflect bullets, and both sides had taken prisoners. Several had been sent back by the Japanese army with all four limbs cut off.

"For heaven's sake, give me mercy," the mutilated soldiers had cried. "Let me have another bullet, please!" And Grandpa, the regiment commander, finally did as they requested. Then his soldiers returned the same number of Japanese prisoners—with the same treatment.

Such nasty tales often metamorphosed into heroic sagas, and people were hypnotized by such heroism. With the distance of time, they could easily overlook the brutality, the suffering, and the human tragedy. I know that I did at the time.

For some reason I have never been clear about, Grandpa, a Nationalist brigade commander by the end of World War Two, secretly joined the Communists in 1946. Perhaps, like many others, he was disgusted by the corruption and incompetence of the Nationalist government; or perhaps he was persuaded that the Communists represented a better future. Those were the most common reasons for the widespread defection of Nationalist soldiers that took place after the war.

Grandpa occasionally talked passionately about one of his best friends, Guo Ren, who he credited with introducing him to Communism. Guo was a talented Communist organizer. In the 1920s, he obtained one of the earliest law degrees in China, and then went to Japan for military training in the Japanese War College. He was probably one of those idealistic intellectuals who searched heaven and earth for the means to reform China. Guo secretly recruited Grandpa into the Communist Party, even as both of them remained Nationalist officers.

I have no idea what Grandpa did after he joined the Communists, but I do know that he was exposed and arrested in early 1948, and a Nationalist military court sentenced him to death.

Unselfish, caring, brave, honest, and trustworthy, Grandpa always made friends wherever he was. Although he was a quiet man, he was a charismatic person who genuinely loved people. He won favor with several of the prison guards as well as the warden. Grandpa and the warden reportedly joined hands in a secret ritual, and became blood brothers.

Days before the scheduled execution, a prison break occurred. More than one hundred prisoners, led by Grandpa, fled with a group of guards and their guns. They escaped to the nearby mountains and became guerrilla soldiers. Guo Ren was the Communist commissar of the entire troop, but he met a horrible death later that year after he was captured by Nationalist troops. His executioners set him on fire and watched him burn for half an hour.

Whenever Grandpa mentioned his dead friend, tears filled his eyes. Perhaps Guo's fate gave him the will to live, no matter what hardship he faced. Curiously, however, only Guo's name was recorded in the Communist Party's official records. Though he recruited many people, Grandpa included, their names were not officially listed as Party members. Although he fought many battles for the Communists, Grandpa's Party membership was not recognized until the 1980s, when membership was no longer much cherished, at least by Grandpa.

To be fair, the Communist government that came to power in 1949 did give Grandpa a salary. A very generous one, in fact. He was appointed a senior consultant to the Hunan Provincial government, a position with much prestige, little work, and no power.

For his part, Grandpa never pursued power. He liked his friends and did everything possible to help them. He let them stay in his apartment, gave them money if they needed it, and provided them with food. Many such friends were his officers and soldiers. Some of his guests were former prison guards who had helped him escape. They got into political trouble, a likely fate for anyone who formerly worked for the Nationalists during those years. Unable to stand the persecution, a few of them went into hiding at Grandpa's place, a misguided tactic that ran them all afoul of the household registration system.

This system, introduced in the mid-1950s by the Communist government, was essentially a restrictive, apartheid-like system that kept rural and urban populations separate. It was also a monitoring system. Residents were required to report and register their guests to neighborhood committees. Otherwise, guests could be driven out or taken away. There was also a very strict limit—sometimes one week, sometimes two—on how long a guest might stay. Overstaying the limit would cause trouble for both the host and the guest. People from the neighborhood committees or neighborhood police stations—each neighborhood had one—would drop by, check on the background of the guest, and then contact the authorities in his or her hometown. If the guest happened to be classified as a "bad" person, he or she would be sent away immediately. Hotels also required that a guest show a permit from his or her work unit or the local authorities before they would offer up a room or a bed. Even sleeping on the street or in a park was not possible, since the neighborhood patrols showed up even there a few times a day.

Grandpa violated the rules. In the 1960s, he took in a few friends who had been accused of being counterrevolutionaries. He did not have the heart to turn them in, and refused to report these ostensible enemies of the state to the authorities. When they were caught—and eventually they all were—Grandpa made all possible efforts to defend them. He claimed he would never turn his back on his friends, especially friends who had saved his life. As a consequence, he was named an enemy of the state himself, and he lost his job.

He also lost his urban residence permit. As an enemy of the state, he was sent back to his village for "reform through hard labor." His family, which included Grandma and his four grandchildren, were also ordered to leave with him, since he was the male head of the household. We all lost our urban residency with all its attendant privileges, such as food ration coupons and basic housing.

On a cold and rainy autumn day, my grandparents and my siblings, carrying a few boxes of belongings, were put on a bus and headed for Grandpa's home village.

STORY TEN: INTERMISSION BETWEEN CITY LIGHTS

My grandparents and their four grandchildren settled in one small room in my grandpa's home village in the central part of Hunan Province.

It was a village of rice farmers. Most people were members of the Gong clan and shared our family name. Grandpa was the second of thirteen siblings, and his father was the eldest son in that family. As a result, most villagers ranked higher than my siblings and me on the lineage ladder. We had "uncles" and "aunts," and even "great aunts" and "great uncles," who were more or less our own age. They would all just be called cousins in English, but the traditional Chinese lineage system—which runs principally through the male lines—categorized kinship differently.

The system was strange to city people like us. I would never call anyone my age anything other than his or her given name. Luckily for me, since I did not speak the local dialect, I could pretend I did not understand anything. And in truth, I understood very little.

Before I had any comprehension of what was happening, my kid brother and I were sent to the village elementary school. It was a bizarre experience. The two-room school had about eighty students in four grades. Some were significantly older—fifteen or sixteen—than most of us. The first- and third-graders sat in one room, the second- and fourth-graders in the other. Two teachers, a man and a woman in their forties, took turns teaching each class. While class was in session for half of the pupils in one classroom, the other half—students in the other grade—would be assigned homework.

The teachers lived at the school. Each of their bedrooms was attached to a classroom. At lunchtime, students took out whatever they had brought with them, and the teachers went back to their rooms and cooked for themselves. Their hot food always smelled wonderful. But the students had their chance to cook, too. On cold winter days, everyone would bring a charcoal burner with them. We all used them as food warmers.

I was assigned to the fourth grade. Having been brought from one of the best schools in a big city to this odd place, I was totally confused, and to make matters worse, I could not understand a word the teachers said. When I looked at the textbooks, each of which was shared by three or four students, I recognized the contents, however. Apparently, the fourth grade here was learning what I had learned in second grade in the city.

Homework was not done on paper, but on a writing board. Teachers did not even look at our homework, let alone report to our parents or grandparents. The only purpose of schooling seemed to be to keep the kids occupied, and to teach them basic reading skills. Most girls and some boys left school permanently after four years. The middle school was far, far away—a two-hour walk. Things like libraries and bookstores were never heard of.

Once I appreciated the realities of my new environment, I was overwhelmed with sadness. I had always loved books—but not schooling—and now I found myself longing for my old school. The village had no electricity and no running water. But what really bothered me was the loneliness, the emptiness, and, worst of all, the feeling of powerlessness. My life was totally beyond my control. Whatever I wanted and whatever I did were irrelevant to what happened. Submission was my only choice, if you could call that a choice.

Somehow, I was able to re-create books I had read in my mind. The stars were so bright in the night country sky. I imagined many earths like ours out there where life was different. It would be much more colorful and there would be so much more happiness. I felt a strong sense that the life I was living belonged to someone else, that one day I would be far, far away from these awful surroundings, and that great adventures were waiting for me in the future.

My dreams, however, were suddenly interrupted one day by my grandma's screaming.

This was the Grandma I never really got to know. A short woman with bound feet, she spoke only Hunan dialect, which I could barely understand, but she was not originally from a rural area. In fact, she had been born into a wealthy family in the rich ancient city of Yangzhou in Jiangsu Province. My father occasionally whispered something about her unhappy life. Her own mother had died when she was little. The stepmother wanted to get rid of her, and soon married her off to a cousin, my grandpa, who lived in a remote rural village a couple of provinces away. She must have had her own dreams as a young girl, but when I met her, she was already a somewhat deranged little woman. She kept mumbling something barely audible, and no one paid attention to her—not even her husband.

One night, weeks after we were driven out of the city, she suddenly began screaming, crying, and singing. Once she started, she would not stop. I never knew she had such a high-pitched voice. As she wailed, she sang a heartbreaking song:

"My son ... My dear son ... Why did you abandon me? You are so cruel ... Your mama is suffering ... My son ... Come back, my dear son ..."

She must be calling for father, I thought. But later I learned she was actually crying out for her beloved younger son, who had died from typhoid fever in 1947. Except for my grandpa and my sister, who she had raised, she did not recognize anyone in the family.

"Go away," she yelled at my brothers and me, "I want my son!"

We could not stay away, for we had the duty of watching her and informing the adults if she started doing anything harmful or dangerous. She did not. She just kept crying and singing.

The children in the village found all this very amusing.

"Look! Look! There is a mad woman!" they ran around and announced to anyone passing by.

With unusual enthusiasm, boys ran around the village and announced this to everyone. These kids—many of whom wore no clothes at all when the weather turned warm—gathered around our house. They applauded my grandma's singing in order to provoke her to do more of it.

"Listen, listen, the mad woman is singing!"

"One more time! Do it one more time!" they applauded at any intermission.

Sometimes someone from outside would throw a stone. If it hit inside, applause and cheering would explode from the crowd. Adults were watching. They seemed to enjoy this, too. A mad woman who sang—what wonderful entertainment in the otherwise dull life of the village!

It was, of course, humiliating to us. During the daytime, Grandpa, who was in his mid-sixties, had to do hard labor in the field. We children had to take turns watching Grandma. My sister, eleven at the time, had the duty of staying in bed with her at night, since she was the only child the old woman recognized.

In the middle of the night, my sister screamed. Grandma had awakened and scratched her a few times. My sister jumped out of the bed. She immediately grabbed a pen and wrote to our parents. She described the situation and then said, "I am becoming a night guard. Please find a way to help us."

Father asked Grandpa to send us to live with our great aunt, Grandpa's elder sister, as a temporary arrangement. Perhaps taking pity on us, the local authorities granted our request and gave us permission to stay temporarily.

Great aunt's house was located in the nearby town. She was already raising six grandchildren of her own; the four of us made the total number ten. Our ages ranged from three to fifteen years old—the age of unruliness.

Great aunt, in her late sixties, was a widow. In fact, she was in her second widowhood. Her first husband had died when she was in her mid-twenties. Following the traditions of the time, she prepared herself for a lifetime of widowhood. But Grandpa, a young military officer, was more broadminded. He went back to his family and persuaded their parents to allow her to remarry.

At the time, however, no decent gentry's family would take in a widow. It was bad luck, to say the least. So great aunt married a businessman who owned a small workshop that produced bean curd, although it was considered a marriage beneath her station at that time.

Still tall and slim in her seventies, great aunt had once been a famous local beauty. She had only two daughters. The older one married a Nationalist military colonel in the 1940s, and the younger one married a Communist military officer in the early 1950s.

Chinese lives in the twentieth century were inevitably intertwined with history and politics, however, and there was really no escape. The Nationalist son-in-law was sent to a labor camp in 1950. His wife waited with their two sons. Many years later, he was released and sent to Guizhou, a remote province, to work in a coal mine. The wife joined her husband there, and gave birth to three more children.

The fate of the Communist military officer son-in-law was only slightly better. He was accused of being a rightist in 1957, and was severely demoted. Because the daughters had too much work on their hands, great aunt ended up taking care of six grandchildren.

Ten children from three families under one roof was quite an experience. In some ways, my great aunt reminded me of my dearest grandma in Guangzhou. She was warm and caring, but firm and fair. For the first time, I got to know my siblings better. And I really loved my cousins. We got along well and formed a large extended family.

The only real problem was food. Rice and other grains were rationed, and children received less than adults. We could afford meat only once a week. At each meal, great aunt would divide the food evenly among all the children, taking only the minimum for herself.

It was a peaceful time—a very short peace before a big storm. Unfortunately, the Great Proletarian Cultural Revolution was approaching.

Story Eleven: Circus Without Bread

I was struck down by typhoid fever in the spring of 1966. When I recovered, the entire nation entered an even more feverish state: the Cultural Revolution.

In a small town like the one in which we lived, the storm of the Cultural Revolution came on with a kind of surreal quality. At first, the circus came. Or rather, the Chinese equivalent of the circus.

The only movie theater in town stopped showing the one or two feature films. "The bourgeois intellectuals and the revisionists in the Party" had made those films, the Party informed viewers. Instead, theaters around the country presented only one show: Chairman Mao, wearing his military outfit, waving to millions of young Red Guards parading on Tiananmen Square.

"Long live Chairman Mao," the Red Guards on the screen shouted for hours on end. When Mao's motorcade passed by, the shouting turned into frantic screaming, accompanied by tears of extreme joy.

The entire nation shared in the frenzy through movie theaters, which lowered ticket prices from ten to eight cents. However, only outcasts actually needed to pay. All work units and neighborhood committees distributed the tickets to "the people"—namely, residents minus the "bad classes"—for free.

"Long live Chairman Mao," everyone shouted along with the Red Guards in our town theater. No one dared not to. But shouting was not the only thing that was imitated.

"Look, that person is crying!" someone whispered.

Soon, tears made their way into many people's eyes. After one typical hour-long film, many theatergoers left with red eyes, publicly displaying their deep affection for the Chairman. People observed one another inside and outside of the theater. Those who managed to shed tears would proudly record this fact in the reports about their own thoughts they made to their own Party leaders.

"So-and-so was with me. He can verify my story," they sometimes claimed, hoping someone had been watching. And of course, someone was always watching—friends, neighbors, colleagues, and family members.

A seditious thought came into my mind more than once. Where had all the tears come from? Were they for real? I, for one, tried my best, but tears refused to fall. I wasn't moved at all by all that shouting and the flamboyant display of emotion. I'd be much more likely to be moved by, say, Pushkin, my favorite writer and poet at the time.

I was never very convinced of Mao's "charismatic power." How could a guy who seldom smiled and was not very articulate in public be charismatic? Similarly, why would a funny little man with a funny mustache like Hitler, or a stocky peasant like Stalin, be appealing? Were people reacting to the deadly power of these men more than their charisma? Could fear be the true cause of all the shouting, crying, and excitement? These were not my thoughts at the age of ten, but they certainly have occurred to me in the years since then.

The revolutionary frenzy was contagious. Soon after the Red Guards paraded in front of Mao in Tiananmen Square in August 1966, parades suddenly appeared in this one-street town every day and every night. They began from opposite sides of the town, passed each other in the middle, and returned to their starting points after half an hour. The street was never empty.

"The Greatest News: Chairman Mao has sent his Red Guards to mobilize us!" This was posted on every public wall in the town. Red flags, drums, marchers ... This once-sleepy town was reaching the boiling point.

Young students from Beijing and other big cities were very visible in the crowd. They spoke differently and looked very urban. And many of them sported trendy, worn-out military uniforms, a proud display of the military connections of their families. For a few months, middle school and college students—unless they bore the burden of "bad" family backgrounds—were given free train and bus tickets to wander around the country and "set off the fire of the Cultural Revolution," according to the Party propaganda machine. Local governments were ordered to arrange lodging and provide food for them. It was actually a happy time for so many youngsters who would otherwise have had no opportunity to travel.

The best attraction in town at the time were the "Mao Zedong thought propaganda teams" formed mostly by young students. These teams, usually consisting of two or three dozen teenagers, would sing and dance and perform short plays, making the collective insanity all the more colorful. The most-performed play ran for fifteen minutes and featured a girl singing a song, condemning the "miserable old days," telling a young girl's story of parents being killed by landlords and of being forced to do hard labor at a young age. Dozens of local girls performed the play, but only one girl got it right—she shed tears each time the story line reached the death of the parents. She sang:

"The dreadful old days

All poor people hated them with blood and tears

The blood, the hatred

Now are gathering in my heart ..."

The team with which she performed became the most popular. "The girl who knows how to cry is coming," children ran around and announced.

With all the singing and dancing, it took the team two hours to go from one end of the street to the other. It thus performed its full program five times every day. Having become a local celebrity, the poor girl was obligated to shed real tears five times a day. What talent! What a show!

Schools stopped teaching. Shops stopped selling. Factories stopped producing. Except for the poor peasants, who had no choice but to take care of their crops, people were having a good time. Some people, anyway.

Had all of this not been so frightening, it would have been very comical. Students from Beijing—the dark princes with their worn-out uniforms and their "good" family backgrounds—not only brought with them songs and parades; they also brought the "red terror." Party propaganda urged people to wipe out the "four olds"—old thinking, old culture, old customs, and old habits—and to pursue "continuous revolution." Encouraged by Mao, the teenage offspring of high-ranking party leaders—mostly high school age—organized themselves as "Red

Guards," a Chinese equivalent of the "brown shirts." They aimed to destroy anything they branded as "old."

Rumors reached this small town that many old temples and famous relics had been smashed and discarded in Beijing and other big cities. And the campaign was to be expanded to the entire country. Our area, one of the ancient centers of Chinese civilization, was full of priceless relics, and soon enough, these rumors were no longer rumors. Red guards from Beijing and other big cities led the charge to ransack Buddhist and Taoist temples and the houses of some local "landlords"—people who had owned and rented out land before the Communist takeover in 1949.

Among the first victims was a small comic book rental shop, a favorite hangout for local kids. The owner had hundreds of books, and he used to charge people one cent per comic book to read them on site. My siblings and cousins loved them all, especially those about ancient legends.

One cent does not sound like much, but it was a huge amount for us, since each of us got an allowance of only twenty cents a month. A popsicle cost three cents. A roasted sweet potato cost two cents, and we were more or less hungry all the time. Spending one cent for the privilege of reading a short comic book was thus definitely a luxury. After handing over the coin, we sat down and slowly absorbed tales of the ancient emperors, heroes, the legendary Monkey King, the Pig Monster, and the funny tramps. We devoured all the words and memorized all the scenes. When we had no money, we peeked over other readers' shoulders, and felt we had gotten something for nothing whenever we were able to see the pictures. Those sweet moments were etched into our young minds, so much so that my kid brother and I can still smell the paper forty years later when we talk about that store.

One hot day in August 1966, all the books in that store were burned by the Red Guards, following the general instructions of Chairman Mao to destroy old things. From hundreds of meters away, we could see the flames and smoke. Burning pages flew into the air. Children ran around chasing them, trying to catch relics of a dying culture, to preserve even a tiny fragment of the fading memory of happy moments.

The bookstore was no more.

Nor were the Buddhist and Taoist temples which had been there for generations. They, too, were all smashed to pieces.

Nervousness spread through the town. Although the town was small, it had existed for three thousand years. Almost every family owned *something* old. Early one morning in late August, a young girl carrying water from the riverbank spotted a small bronze Buddha, abandoned in the midst of some stones, and she picked it up. Word on the street was that the girl, who came from a very poor family, was able to sell the Buddha for a princely sum—four yuan.

Meanwhile, other valuable objects—religious items, ancient paintings, and books—were cropping up around town, discarded by frightened people in the middle of the night. And the entire young population began to engage in what seemed like a great treasure hunt. One morning, a group of kids found a large number of Qing Dynasty bronze coins at the bottom of the river. Within an hour, hundreds of children jumped in, diving and searching, hoping to make a fortune. The ten of us all participated, but lady luck eluded us.

The trash dealers now remained open for longer hours. They bought such things from children. The bronze items were particularly sought after. They would be sent off to be melted down and remade as industrial products, including bullets. No adults dared to be part of this enterprise, though. Neighborhood committees ordered all those with suspicious class backgrounds to report in. A list of targets for the Red Guards—slated for punishments ranging from house-ransacking to detention—was compiled in each neighborhood.

Eventually, a group of local Red Guards, wearing their signature red armbands, came to my great aunt's house.

"What is your class background?" the head of the group demanded.

"Middle class," great aunt answered.

"Middle class? Doesn't that mean capitalist?"

"We had a very small business before Liberation," great aunt replied calmly.

At that, ten young students—none older than fifteen or sixteen—rushed in. They turned over everything in the house, looking for items indicative of a "bourgeois lifestyle" or anything reminiscent of "the old days." They broke a few cups and bowls and knocked on our walls looking for secret compartments, but could not find many valuables. We were poor.

"What is this?" A Red Guard picked up a piece of silk, which had been a birthday present from my father to my great aunt.

"Silk," she said.

"This indicates a capitalist lifestyle! We are taking it away!"

They later found a pair of high-heeled shoes left there by one of great aunt's daughters, and a few other minor items. And they took the only science book we had. Fortunately for me, I had already memorized every word in the book.

With all our valuable property in hand, they left after two hours. We dared not ask where the guards came from, or what they were going to do with our property. Some would be destroyed, such as the high-heeled shoes; others would become someone else's private property. The entire house was left in a huge mess. Everything was upside down.

Before leaving, the leader of the group pointed at our empty walls and said, "You have only one picture of Chairman Mao here! This shows your true class feelings! Fix this! We will come back later and check!" So the next day, we spent a small fortune we could ill afford on a dozen Mao portraits and hung them around the house. We could not even say that we "bought" Mao's portraits. Instead, every customer, willing or unwilling, had to say that they "invited" the "cherished portraits of the Great Leader" into their homes. A few ill-informed customers used the word "buy." Immediately, nearby Red Guards—they seemed to be everywhere, and always watching—rushed in, demanding information about their class background. If the answer was one of the "bad classes," chances were that person would be beaten, or at least publicly condemned.

We prayed those people would not come back; but if they did, we were prepared. We were lucky. Even the most vicious of the Red Guards could not find much glory in persecuting an old lady and ten children. They never came back.

The situation degenerated rapidly from there. Many school teachers—convenient targets of angry students—were beaten and tortured. The most persecuted ones, however, were the so-called "five black classes": landlords, rich peasants, counterrevolutionaries, "bad elements" (usually convicted criminals), and rightists.

The street propaganda performances now gave way to parades of public humiliation organized by the Red Guards. The targets, always wearing paper dunce caps and sometimes a sign bearing their names and ostensible crimes hanging around their necks, were lined up on the street. One or two were forced to strike a gong—or a metal washbasin if a gong was not available—to mark every step in the parade. Following each strike, all the targets would be required to shout out:

"I am an ox-ghost and a snake-monster!"

"I am guilty of being an enemy of the people!"

"I am guilty, and I will repay my debt to the people!"

"I deserve death ten thousand times! I should be sent to the lowest level of hell!"

My great aunt's son-in-law, the Communist who had been accused of being a rightist and who was the father of two of my cousins, was among the targets. His head was bent way down on his chest in humiliation, for he must have guessed that his children were watching.

Once a woman was among the targets. Two worn-out shoes hung on each side of one of her shoulders. Large characters were written on her dunce cap: "broken shoes." That was a Chinese insult signifying a woman who had had extramarital affairs. She lowered her head so much that a small child like me could catch only a glimpse of her face—it was as white as a sheet of paper. Stories like hers naturally caused excitement—her infidelity was recounted again and again, with many details and in many different versions. It became the best entertainment in town.

Soon, bodies of suicides began to be seen floating on the river from which we obtained our drinking water. It was, indeed, a red terror.

STORY TWELVE: IT SMELLED OF MORTALITY

Grandpa came to visit us less and less frequently. Soon, he stopped coming. Later, we learned he had been detained by Red Guards who came to the village looking for "bad classes" to attack. No place was too remote for them.

The whole nation was in chaos. The Red Guards, with their "good" family backgrounds, went after their teachers, the "bad classes," and whoever else they did not like. Death reports—killing by Red Guards or suicides caused by their actions—came from every corner of the country, as the entire nation sank into a sea of blood and terror. So when Mao suddenly had a change of heart in November 1966 and asked the "people" to rise against the "capitalist roaders inside the Party," that is, Party leaders who had retained some common sense or who Mao did not like, people responded violently. Many seized the moment and formed "rebel" groups to target those in positions of authority and privilege. Government officials were widely attacked. They were treated the same way their children—the Red Guards—had treated others. The Communist officials now had to take some of their own medicine. Then the Red Guards and the rebels—who sometimes also adopted the name "Red Guards," which made things all the more confusing—started to fight each other.

That was how two years of chaos and civil war began.

At the end of December 1966, my parents finally decided to take the eldest three of their four children back to Guangzhou. Taking advantage of the chaotic situation, they were able to persuade a low-ranking officer in the local police department to register us as residents. If the administrative system had been functioning normally, this would have been utterly impossible.

The Red Guards were still traveling around the country, but now the so-called "rebels" joined them. Millions of people—mostly young, but some not so young any more—were touring the country for free. The three of us—twelve, ten and a half, and eight and a half years old—took a bus and later squeezed into a train, all by ourselves.

The train was unimaginably crowded. Above us were the dangling feet of those who sat on the luggage shelves. We children sat on the laps of a few men. Under the seats was another layer of human bodies. The toilet was also full of people, so better forget trying to use it. Whenever the train stopped, we immediately took turns going outside for a bathroom break; whoever remained inside took on the duty of saving our seats, or rather, our laps.

What was normally an eight-hour train ride took three full days.

The city I had left more than a year ago felt very different. Guangzhou, or Canton, had always had a cosmopolitan atmosphere. Even under the Communists, residents there were more interested in food and entertainment than Party politics. Their history, their distinct dialect, their softer and lighter local music, their famous delicacies, and their special connections to the outside world had all made the Cantonese people the object of far more Party suspicion than those in other areas. In 1956, in fact, the Party had launched a campaign that effectively expelled almost all Cantonese-speaking cadres from key government positions, replacing them with Mandarin speakers.

Consequently, most work units—schools, government offices, factories, etc.—ended up with Mandarin-speaking Party leaders and Cantonese-speaking subordinates. While the Cantonese usually had some sense of what the Mandarin-speakers were saying—Mandarin, after all, was the official language of China, and was taught in schools throughout the country—the opposite was not true, for the latter rarely learn to understand Cantonese, a notoriously difficult dialect to master. Even the children of these Party leaders who grew up in Canton usually refused to speak the dialect, considering it low class. Mandarin-speaking thus became a sign of status related to Communist rule.

The rift between the Mandarin-speaking Party propaganda machine and the more entertaining and consumer-oriented Cantonese culture had made Guangzhou an unusual and fun city in the 1960s. That was the Guangzhou I remembered. But it was a different city now. Shop windows were covered with "big character posters" that carried political messages. These posters, denouncing particular individuals and groups in frightening language, now covered every inch of the public walls.

"So-and-so, if you do not surrender, we will smash your dog head into pieces!"

"Burn so-and-so! Fry him in a hot pot!"

"We will break so-and-so down and crush him with one foot!"

The names were those of disgraced teachers, school officials, local cadres, and others unfortunate enough to have run afoul of those who wrote the posters. I recognized some of them. They included some of our neighbors, denounced by their own students.

The streets, formerly clean, were now littered with fragments of decaying posters. Pieces with frightening words like "smash," "crush," "down with," "fry," and "burn," together with various people's names, blew through the air, eventually piling up on street corners.

My parents did not look happy when they met us. Soon we understood why. When I got home, I noticed that at least half of the books from our bookshelves were missing. Later I learned that Red Guards from mother's school had come with a truck. They had taken all the books they were able to carry and burned them in public.

"May I see Grandma soon?" I quickly asked.

When I was told that Grandma was away, sadness overwhelmed me. Oh, how I missed her! But was she really away? And when would she come back? Then I heard what had really happened.

As a former landlord, Grandma had been sent back to live in her village, which she had left as a teenager. Her property—the apartment building in which she lived and in which I had grown up—had been confiscated. She had been deprived of her livelihood and her urban residency. Eventually, in the 1970s, she was allowed to come back, but she never uttered a word about how she survived during those years.

Grandma was not the only person missing in the family. I also didn't see my aunt, my mother's younger sister.

Auntie was a military doctor. Young and beautiful, with raven black hair and smiling round eyes, she had had a promising medical career. Her husband, a 1956 college graduate, was sent to study economics at Moscow University. He had returned to China and was working as the assistant to the provincial propaganda boss. Thus the couple had some access to the "inner circle."

It took me a while to figure out what had happened to my aunt. She was in jail.

In August 1966, the red terror was spreading. Leading the charge was Mao's wife, Jiang Qing, backed by Mao himself, of course. Jiang once described herself as merely "Mao's dog," without any real power of her own.

Jiang, a Shanghai movie actress who turned Communist in the late 1930s, married Mao in 1946. A neurotic woman, she was despised by many veteran Communist leaders. Her many love affairs before she met the chairman made her a joke among Mao's comrades. Rumor had it that the Politburo had passed a resolution when Mao abandoned his third wife—a veteran revolutionary soldier who went through all the hardships with her husband in the 1930s, including walking the entire route of the famous "Long March"—and married Jiang. It banned Jiang from participating in politics for the next twenty years. If so, the time was up. Jiang was unleashed by Mao to get at his political rivals. Her hatred of the veteran Communist cadres caused her to demand blood—and the more the better. Millions of ordinary people fell victim, because the entire purge campaign was launched under the mantle of "searching for class enemies" in the society.

My aunt learned about Jiang's background from her husband, and told the story to her best friend. The "best friend," in turn, reported what she had said to the military authorities.

And in September 1966, my thirty-four-year-old aunt, five months pregnant with my cousin, was arrested for "spreading vicious rumors against Chairman Mao and Comrade Jiang Qing."

"What was the origin of these rumors?" her interrogators demanded.

She refused to answer, protecting her husband. She held off for several months, although a connection could easily have been made between the two of them. She was willing to pay a dire price for her family. However, her husband could not hold out much longer. He went to the authorities, confessed that he was the source of the rumor, and accused his wife of twisting his words into a political attack. He denounced her, and asked for a divorce.

With this new information in hand, the interrogators put my aunt on the spot again.

"Your husband has already confessed. He also demanded a divorce, since you are such a sadistic counterrevolutionary."

At this, my aunt fainted. She just fell apart, and gave birth prematurely to a baby girl, of whom she got only a glimpse before the newborn was taken and sent to her father.

The military court handed down an eight-year sentence to my aunt. She appealed, which was permitted under the law but which proved to be another unwise move. Since her appeal was clear evidence of her refusal to admit guilt, she was given an *additional* five years. Thirteen years altogether, for telling the truth about Mao's wife in private. The following decade, she was sent off to a prison camp to do hard labor.

Truth be told, being sent to jail might not have been all that bad a fate at that particular time. The most extreme forms of torture and humiliation occurred outside of prisons, and were conducted by teenage high school students.

About twenty schoolteachers lived in our building. All were college graduates from the 1940s and 1950s who were teaching in high schools within a three-mile radius. This area was also home to the headquarters of the Guangzhou Military Zone and the Guangdong Provincial Government, and as a result, many offspring of high-ranking military officers and civilian officials attended those schools. When the Cultural Revolution was launched, these students became the early Red Guards. They were the most vicious. They detained teachers they did not like, beat them, and even killed some.

Mother was one of the targets at her school. The Red Guard leading the charge against her was a student in her English class. The year before, that particular student, whose father was a military officer, wrote down only one line on his English exam: *Long live Chairman Mao!* Then he left the exam room.

Mother failed him, as any teacher would have done.

"She failed me because I wrote down 'Long live Chairman Mao,'" he asserted. "This shows her true hatred of the great chairman!"

That was a deadly allegation. Everyone could see that it was ridiculous, but no one dared dispute it. That was what "revolution" meant. Mother was put in the detention center at her school. The Red Guards—her former students—ransacked our house, took away many things, and smashed many more.

At another school, Father was severely beaten by his students. A strong man and an amateur *kung fu* master, he avoided severe injury by protecting his head with both hands. But the worst story was of a female math teacher who lived upstairs. She came from a landlord family. Her Red Guard students claimed that they had to "correct" her bad lifestyle. The teenagers—boys and girls alike—shaved her curly hair on one side of her head, leaving the other side uncut, which was humiliating, and put her through every kind of torture they could imagine.

"They forced manure and trash into my mouth," she recalled years later, still trembling visibly at the thought.

Some teachers were beaten to death or committed suicide. No one dared mention them. Four decades later, a friend of mine, whose father was also a teacher at the time, interviewed teachers and students from 118 middle schools around China. She found out that thirty teachers had been beaten to death in those schools.

More often than not, the beating and killing occurred in public. In fact, demonstrating to the public how much power they had was exactly the point the Red Guards were trying to make with their excessive brutality. They were showing that they were destined to inherit total political power from their parents, and they were consummating that inheritance through violence. They were having fun. If a few people were killed along their road to power, so be it.

STORY THIRTEEN: A SLAP ON MY FACE

For a year and half—from the spring of 1967 to the fall of 1968—China was in great turmoil.

The original Red Guards were attacked by newly rising rebels. The rebels overthrew local governments and seized power from them, only to be attacked by the conservatives, veteran party activists mobilized by the deposed local officials to defend themselves against the rebels. Then the military began to get involved, often seizing power itself or in alliance with some local Party leaders. The conflicts soon escalated from words to fists to clubs, and eventually to guns. All the factions acquired guns from the People's Liberation Army in one way or another—either directly or through subterfuge.

All the factions were fighting in the name of Chairman Mao. All swore to wipe out "class enemies." The only issue in contention was *whom* to label as such enemies. It was unbridled urban warfare. Armed gangs paraded through the streets every day, carrying the dead bodies of their own heroes and demanding revenge. Gangs in Guangzhou had relatively easy access to the military arsenal: trains carrying weapons from China to North Vietnam passed through the area every day. Train schedules would be passed along by insiders to their comrades outside, who would then stage train robberies.

Guangzhou looked like Beirut in the 1980s or Baghdad in 2007. The school compound in which our apartment building was located was turned into a fortress by armed student gangs. Guns in hand, these teenagers sped around in Jeeps—also acquired from the military—and shot bullets into the air just for fun. We children stayed indoors as much as we could. Every day, we would see new posters or flyers with names and sometimes photos, indicating that more people had been killed in the war. Each faction would name their own dead "revolutionary martyrs." More battles were launched for revenge, and more people died.

In the summer of 1968, a rumor began floating around Guangzhou that criminals in a nearby jail had organized a successful prison break and escaped into the city. All neighborhoods were supposed to organize and report any strangers. Our building's neighborhood committee reached a collective decision to close all entrances, including sealing all first-floor windows with bricks. Even the main entrance was partially sealed, with only a hole 1.5 feet across and 6 feet high to permit residents to enter and to exit. (It was lucky that we never had a fire during that period.) Our committee also decided to organize our own guard force. All adults and children over seven were paired up to guard the front entrance twenty-four hours a day, seven days a week. Each shift included one adult and one child. The earliest started at 3:00 a.m. If the guards discovered something suspicious, they were supposed to strike a metal washbasin to wake everyone up.

Children were somewhat excited at being assigned the same duty as the adults.

"We need weapons!" someone suggested.

My kid brother, barely ten at the time (he later became an engineer at GE and Motorola), took charge of making our weapons. He found a few used knives and long iron nails, sharpened them, and tied the objects onto wooden sticks, bayonet-style. Our primitive ancestors would have been proud. Our weapons looked much like their ancient hunting tools, except for their iron heads.

The basin alarms sounded a few times at night, but not much happened until one hot and sticky night. The clattering of the basin again woke the residents. This time it seemed different, because the noise lasted for quite a while.

Many adults came out. I followed them quietly; I didn't want to miss the excitement. A big crowd had already gathered in the dining hall. I climbed through the window and took a peek inside.

Over the heads of the crowd, I saw a man tied to a pole. I could only guess his age: late twenties or early thirties, perhaps. He looked kind of dumb, and did not resemble any image I had of a vicious criminal.

A group of seven or eight students were whipping, kicking, and punching him. The guy, who looked very dull, showed little response to the beating. Was this one of the escaped convicts?

Half-standing on the window sill for a while, my legs went numb. Why didn't the guy say something or simply scream? Didn't he feel pain from all that beating? How could that unresponsive guy have been a threat to us?

Suddenly, one of the students took out a knife and stabbed the dull man in the heart. Blood spurted out. A lot of blood. The victim's face lost its reddish color. His head tilted to the left. He died in an instant.

It was easy. Way too easy, the killing.

I ran home, very frightened. It was an animal kind of fear. That face was etched in my mind, appearing each time I closed my eyes. I could not wipe it from my memory.

The dead body was hung on a light pole in a nearby public square for public display for a few weeks, until it eventually fell apart under the hot summer sun of southern China. I had to walk by the area every day to go to the market. I avoided looking at the body, but its smell, the creepiness of being near a body, and, most importantly, the dreadful memory of that night, really haunted me. The memory became the symbol of that horrific era to me.

After the dust settled, we finally learned that the victim was a mentally retarded person, possibly also deaf and dumb. Not realizing the danger, he wandered around late at night and was caught. He could not give his address when asked, nor could he respond to questions such as whether he was an escaped convict. His life was then taken, senselessly.

So were many other human lives. Killing was made so easy during those years.

The coexistence and codependence of anarchy and totalitarianism came to an end in the fall of 1968, when Mao finished ousting his political rivals within the Party and the government, and ordered the military to take over.

The factional fights soon stopped. Most middle school students were sent to the countryside. In Guangzhou, the military detained many faction leaders. All middle school and college teachers were ordered to report to "study classes" in their schools, where the military leaders would sort them out, one after another.

Each school set up a detention center to imprison all "questionable" people. The in-house military leaders—usually at the rank of lieutenant—would hand-pick student activists to be their guards and assistant interrogators. These student activists—always from the "good" families—were spared the fate of being sent to work in rural areas, and were promised better job assignments in urban factories. The designated enemies, on the other hand, were taken from their homes and detained indefinitely. They would no longer earn salaries. In these prisons, they were interrogated, tortured, and dragged out to the public for humiliation. Such detention centers were set up in all schools, factories, government offices, and townships. Millions of people were taken without any due process. Another round of murders and suicides was approaching.

Both of my parents were put in such detention centers. A minimum allowance—the government-established poverty line—was given to each child. The entire sum amounted to about twenty percent of my parents' old salary. The four of us—ages six, ten, twelve, and thirteen—were on our own.

Father, who was accused of being a "Soviet spy" for having worked with the Russian experts in the 1950s, was also an amateur Beijing Opera singer. His interrogators came to us repeatedly, demanding all information about him, including a complete list of his favorite songs. Fortunately, we did not know much.

While we were compiling the song list as the interrogators waited, I thought of one named "When I fight the enemies again," a song sung by a hero in a Beijing opera, and I mentioned it to my sister, who was in charge of keeping the list.

Sixteen months older than me and far more politically shrewd, my sister quickly stepped hard on my foot under the table. I immediately understood I had made a potentially fatal mistake. The song title itself would be enough to convict my father for another terrible crime. Fortunately, the interrogators were examining something else at the time, and did not hear me. This was a major relief.

Father, like Grandpa, was a very social person. He had to be feeling extremely lonely in detention. On his forty-first birthday, I suddenly felt an impulse to show him some affection. I spent all that was left of my monthly allowance, bought a small piece of cake, and went to visit him.

"My child, you remembered my birthday!" Father was moved.

No one remembered my twelfth birthday, though.

My next visit to him wasn't pleasant at all. Father had hypertension, which required medical attention. One day, my sister and I made some soup for him—a stock made with meat and special herbs to help lower his blood pressure. Meat was rationed at the time. Each resident was entitled to 250 grams (a little over half a pound) every month. Before the Cultural Revolution, some necessities, such as grain and clothing, were rationed, but beginning in mid-1968, almost every item needed for daily life was rationed: meat, 250 grams per month per person; clothing, one outfit per year; bean curd, two pieces per month; bathroom tissue, one roll per month. The list went on and on.

The soup was a big deal, since we had to use our own rations for father. I went to his detention place. The guards pointed at the container I was carrying, and demanded to know what was in it.

"Medicine for my father's hypertension," I replied.

They opened the container and discovered the soup.

"What medicine? Is this medicine?!"

"Yes," I insisted.

"You capitalists still want to keep your lifestyle! This is bad! Haven't you learned your lesson yet?"

I kept trying to reason with them. "My father has severe hypertension. This is, indeed, medicine!"

I should have known better. I should have remembered that it was impossible to reason with those guys. It was a stupid move on my part, and would give Father trouble later on.

While I was arguing with them, one guard led father out of his cell. His head was lowered, and his shoulders stooped. He seemed much smaller, and did not look like the authoritarian figure that I knew and feared.

When father raised his head, he saw me arguing with the guards. Then he slapped me, hard, on my face. I was stunned for a few seconds. I heard the guards laughing, but could not make out what they were saying. I left immediately, and never made another trip there.

Whatever willingness I had to submit to authority, of whatever kind, was fast being exhausted.

STORY FOURTEEN: THE DEFINING MOMENT

The last two years of the 1960s witnessed the peak of the Mao cult. The Cultural Revolution had run out of steam. Whatever zeal had existed for revolution had by and large vanished by this point. With massive detentions and regular executions, the military ruled with an iron fist. Fear dominated every corner. Even children learned how to watch their backs.

Terror was the trademark of the Mao cult. Whoever dared utter an unfavorable word against Mao, even unintentionally, would be severely punished.

A female teacher in our neighborhood got a five-year sentence simply because of a careless mistake. At a public rally she attended, participants took turns shouting slogans.

"Long live Chairman Mao!"

"Good health forever to Chairman Mao's successor Vice Chairman Lin Biao!"

"Down with Liu Shaoqi!" (Liu, the former president of China and Mao's political rival, had lost his power in 1966 and died in jail in 1969).

After a few long hours, this teacher got so tired that she accidentally shouted out the wrong words: "Down with Chairman Mao!" And with that, she lost five years of her life to hard labor.

Another neighbor almost lost his life when someone discovered that he used old newspaper to wrap food. That particular piece of paper happened to have Mao's picture on it, as nearly all newspapers did at the time. He was taken from his home and beaten half to death.

Most of us had long since learned to cut the chairman's picture out carefully before using newspaper for anything other than reading.

Mao's portrait was posted in every room, public or private. The "big character" posters disappeared, replaced by slogans in big red characters. Walls were painted red, the color of the Communist Revolution. A "sea of red" was created, with Mao's portrait always commanding center stage. And the country, after years in a pressure cooker, was finally being driven to complete insanity.

Apart from organizing the regular "struggle sessions" at which everyone was required to watch ill-fated "class enemies" be humiliated onstage, the schools had no other activities for students. All teachers were put in "study classes," a euphemism for detention centers. Each school was occupied by a dozen or so soldiers and a team of Party activists from a nearby factory. We mostly stayed at home. We had little money, and my sister and I had to use what we did have to take care of our two younger brothers.

A great deal of our time and energy was spent in lines at the markets. Refrigerators were unheard of. In the hot climate of Guangdong, food had to be purchased fresh and cooked the same day. That became a great challenge for my sister and me. We had limited resources; almost everything was rationed, and even with rationing, food was perpetually in short supply. Every morning before six, one of us had to go to the market and stand in several different lines—one for vegetables, one for bean curd, one for meat, another for fish, and others for toilet paper, rice, and whatever other daily necessities we needed. Each line generally took between thirty minutes and three hours, if not more.

Often children in the neighborhood—if they got along—would help one another by staking out positions in multiple lines. Soon we all became experts in lining up. The tricks included standing in whatever line was forming, regardless of what was being sold. That position was tradable—one was almost guaranteed to find a person in another line who was willing to trade places.

Our two kid brothers were growing fast and needed new clothing. We could not afford new clothing, so we learned how to sew. A few pieces of our parents' old clothes were used as raw material. One day, one brother came home crying.

"The other kids laughed at my clothes! I don't want to wear this!"

He had a point. He was wearing a poorly made jacket with sleeves of two different colors. Unfortunately, that was the only thing available to him.

My only consolation in the midst of such insanity and deprivation was reading. I read whatever I could find. I devoured every word on paper, as long as it was not a current government publication. I simply could not stand the shrill propaganda that the Party was dishing out.

Although almost all books were banned, many still found their way to readers. Neighborhood children quietly circulated forbidden books among themselves. Eager young minds were, in this way, able to absorb some of the knowledge and the tradition that was officially denied them.

One day, I borrowed a small book from a neighbor. It was a thin book of fewer than two hundred pages. The jacket was a plain, dark blue and a simple title appeared on it, without any other design. I immediately recognized it as an "internally circulated" item. Such books were available only to Party cadres above a certain rank. The designation was reserved mostly for important books translated from foreign languages.

The title of the book was *One Day in the Life of Ivan Denisovich*, and it was by Alexander Solzhenitsyn.

Ivan Denisovich Shukhov was an ordinary prisoner in a Soviet labor camp in Siberia. He had fought for his country during the Second World War and was captured by the Germans. After the war, the Soviet government handed him a ten-year sentence, which was in the mid-range of sentences handed out to war prisoners: some got five, others got twenty-five.

The book described a "happy" day in the labor camp. Nothing bad happened; Ivan received a parcel with real meat sausage, survived another day, and was looking forward to the future. It was just an ordinary day in the gulag. Ivan felt lucky.

Solzhenitsyn was a great writer. He attended to every detail, and his writing style was understated, without any trace of the high-pitched propaganda that characterized most Soviet literature. I finished the book within two hours, but it gave me a strange feeling.

The author was clearly telling a miserable story. An innocent person in prison, deprived of his freedom and his family. What could be worse? But why didn't I feel more for the poor guy? Why didn't I have tears in my eyes? Why did I feel that it actually *was* a "lucky day," as the author had sarcastically suggested?

Ivan was, indeed, in jail, but so were several people in my family. Prisoners in Ivan's camp were discussing their feelings, their religious beliefs (which were Russian Orthodox), and their dissatisfaction with their immediate surroundings. They even had a Bible on hand, although the owner had to hide it in a crack in the wall. They also had bread (a rarity in China then) and sometimes meat. Life in that Siberian labor camp was almost *enviable* to a Chinese person in 1968, when uttering one word against the Party would invariably send you to a far worse fate.

That odd feeling prompted me to read the book again. As I reread, I paid more attention to the preface and the footnotes. The preface, written by the Chinese propaganda department that had approved the translation, indicated that the author was a "co-conspirator with the revisionist Khrushchev" in their anti-Stalin scheme. Then I noticed the following passage:

"Somebody in the room was bellowing: 'Old Man Whiskers won't ever let you go! He wouldn't trust his own brother, let alone a bunch of cretins like you!'"

This passage came complete with a footnote that explained what "Old Man Whiskers" meant: "This is a vicious attack against Comrade Stalin."

Lightning struck me. Comrade Stalin? A leader as great as Mao, whose portrait was displayed next to those of Marx, Engels, and Lenin in Tiananmen Square? How could anyone talk about him with such disrespect?

I wasn't completely ignorant of the Great Purge. During the Cultural Revolution, part of Khrushchev's 1956 secret report was circulated as supporting evidence to justify the revolution.

Chairman Mao's "continuous revolution," Party propaganda intoned, was the most effective means to weed out hidden capitalist agents like Khrushchev who had betrayed Stalin after his death. Still, some details of Stalin's horrific Great Purge were revealed, and caught the eye of many Chinese, including me.

To those who live in a normal society, it might be hard to fathom why children as young as twelve would be interested in dense political history and writing. The answer, of course, is that we were forced into adulthood by circumstances. Whether we wanted politics or not, politics controlled our lives.

That day, I read the book over and over. Unlike leftists in the West, I never doubted the facts presented by the author. I knew they were all true. I had witnessed and experienced similar, if not more intense, suffering. I needed only to make the connection between suffering and the entire system, and especially to its "great leaders."

On that day, I made that connection. I came to the conclusion that Stalin was responsible for all the misery described in the book. If it treated innocent people like Ivan so unfairly and cruelly, the Soviet Union was surely a terrible society. And if Russia was terrible, what about China? How about Mao?

It was so frighteningly simple and apparent. This bolt of lightning was a defining moment for me. Suddenly, everything objective became subjective. Unchallengeable faith was shaken. The melancholy of life was transcended into political dissent. From then on, everything originating from the authorities would be subject to examination and scrutiny.

I was at once elated and terrified by this revelation. All the images of ugly "class enemies" from government propaganda started spinning in my head. Was I becoming one of them?

I looked in the mirror. Nothing happened. I waited a little while. Still nothing.

I buried this terrible secret—my thoughts about Mao and the Communist system—deep in my mind. If it was revealed, even inadvertently, I would put everyone around me into a deeper hole. People were executed for having such thoughts.

Over the next few years, I was torn between driving the treasonous thoughts out of my mind and quietly enjoying the guilty pleasure of thinking them. The latter eventually won out. After all, thoughts had lives of their own. After they enter your head, they have a way of putting down roots. They more I tried to drive them out, the more holes I saw in the official teachings.

That day marked a transcendent moment for me. It defined the rest of my life.

STORY FIFTEEN: THOU SHALT NOT BEAR FALSE WITNESS

Housing was always in short supply during the Mao years. Our two-room apartment measured about two hundred square feet. Two bunk beds for the four children occupied most of the space in which we lived. Cooking was done and clothes were washed in the public corridor. Two back-to-back buildings housing eighty families shared a communal bathroom with a few showerheads and toilets. With running water in the house and flush toilets nearby, our living conditions were considered rather good compared to those of most urban residents.

Tight housing made neighborhood surveillance so easy that nothing escaped the eyes of the neighbors. All apartment doors faced the corridor, leaving the activities of all households observable to anyone passing by. One could also see into the windows of several rooms in the next building.

People rarely closed their doors unless they were going to sleep. If someone did, rumors would start to fly. Did that family have something to hide? Particularly, if a woman—a few of them had husbands living in other parts of the country—closed her door too often, people would speculate that she was having an extramarital affair. "Someone is seen to be with someone" was a perpetually fascinating subject to all residents, adults and children alike.

These two buildings had been built as dormitories for young faculty members at a teacher's college. Although the young faculty grew older and had families, they remained there. Very little housing was built in the 1960s and 1970s, when the government marshaled all possible resources to the military and invested in weaponry, including nuclear weapons. When the college was closed in 1962, all residents were reassigned to teach middle school, many in the same locations. Therefore, the neighbors were often also colleagues.

Each time a political campaign was launched, people were commanded by the Party to disclose their past—experience and thoughts alike—and to perform self-criticism in front of other colleagues. Colleagues were also required to criticize one another. After many such political campaigns, everyone's history became an open book. Everyone knew which schools their neighbors went to, in which political campaign they had been criticized, whether they had been condemned as rightists (it seemed a lot of our neighbors had been), or whether they had ever had extramarital affairs. The list went on and on.

The female teacher living in the room next to ours worked at the same school as my father. She was in her mid-thirties. Her two sons had been born in the early 1960s and were the same ages as my younger brothers.

When the Cultural Revolution was launched, that teacher immediately became an active participant, and my father was a convenient target for her. She posted a big character poster near the gate of the school, on which she wrote:

"I am writing to expose Gong, the Soviet agent. He owns many Russian books and reads them every day. He worships the Soviet revisionists. He has also dared to teach his children to do so! He is truly an agent of counterrevolutionary restoration! I denounce him! I also urge every revolutionary to join me in denouncing him!"

And so it went.

Every day, she and her husband passed by our apartment, but they refused to talk to us. Her mother-in-law, an illiterate old lady, had trouble understanding what was going on, so she continued to smile and engage us when her daughter-in-law was not present. The boys of the two rival families still played together sometimes, although the adults did not approve of such an association.

At the dinner table, my parents warned us: "Xie [the neighbor] is actually a rightist. She simply slipped through the net." "Slipped-through rightist" was a name given to those who had been criticized in 1957, but had, fortunately for them, avoided being officially listed as rightists.

Terminology like this was as precise as it was ridiculous. I could write a separate book just to explain the historical background and political meaning of the epithets used at the time. To wit:

"Escaped landlord"—someone whose family had owned land in rural areas, but who left before the Communist takeover.

"Historical counterrevolutionary"—someone who worked for the Nationalist government before the Communist takeover.

"Capitalist running dog"—someone who once worked for a landlord or an entrepreneur.

"Bourgeois reactionary academic authoritarian figure"—someone who was an established scholar.

"Nationalist relic"—someone employed by the Nationalist government before 1949.

"Worn-out shoe"—a woman who had extramarital affairs.

"Family of a counterrevolutionary"—someone with a relative who had been labeled a counterrevolutionary.

"Agents for the imperialists and the revisionists"—someone who had had contact at some point with the West or the Soviet Union.

These were only some of the names applied to people in my neighborhood, and to designated targets around the country as well. Each person might have more than one such label hanging over his head. My father, for example, was, in various quarters, referred to as a "slipped-through rightist," a "bourgeois academic authoritarian figure," and someone whose family member—his father—was a counterrevolutionary.

Our parents told us that Teacher Xie, our neighbor, had been accused of being a rightist in 1957, when she was a college student. She deserved that label, my parents assured me. It was a mistake that she had been able to slip through.

Through the years, I met hundreds of such victims of the Mao regime. Significantly, a very large proportion of them were also Party officials or activists who had victimized others before their own demise. Many, not surprisingly, thought that their victims deserved what they got but that they themselves had been falsely accused and undeservedly persecuted. Instead of denouncing the Party, they blamed the victims. In some cases, being victimized themselves seemed only to *increase* their zeal for victimizing others, a strategy designed to gain approval from the authorities.

In such an environment, not even children were shielded from the politics of victimization. All neighborhood children either were told by their parents, or learned from the big character posters, of allegations against the adults. Since the chaos of the Cultural Revolution lasted for quite a while, no adult was immune from attack. Inevitably, children used such allegations as weapons in dog fights among themselves.

On day in 1968, my brother and I were arguing about something with the neighbor's eight-year-old child. He threw out an allegation:

"Your father is a Soviet agent and a reactionary academic authoritarian figure!"

I was mad and shot back:

"Your mother is a slipped-through rightist!"

We continued in this manner for a while, and eventually the fight ended. But the next day, Teacher Xie grabbed me by the shoulder and dragged me into her room.

"You slandered me!" she hissed.

I stared at her, thinking of what my parents had said about her. She seemed to be reading my mind, and continued: "Your parents are spreading rumors! They attack revolutionaries like me! They should be severely punished!"

After a few seconds, she turned less accusatory and more explanatory. "Everyone makes mistakes when they are young. I made a mistake, but your parents committed a crime! Your family harbored a counterrevolutionary!"

I suddenly realized that *she* might have been the cause—or at least one of the causes—of a recent tragedy in my family. My grandfather in Hunan had been taken from his village and severely beaten by Red Guards. He escaped and came to live with us for a few months. Then, on New Year's Day in 1968, a group of people came from Hunan and took my grandpa away, right in front of us. My parents were thus accused of "harboring a counterrevolutionary." Was Xie the one who reported my grandpa? My family never learned the truth. Grandpa was put in solitary confinement for the next several years.

Relationships among neighbors deteriorated even further in the fall of 1968, when all the adults were ordered to leave their families and attend "study classes," which turned out to be detention centers or labor camps. But there were differences in how they were treated. Some, like my parents, were categorized as "enemies." They were not allowed to go home at all, and they stopped receiving salaries. Others were classified as "intellectuals who need reeducation." They were forced to engage in self-criticism and hard labor by day, but were allowed to go home on some weekends; they also continued to receive their pay. Teacher Xie was in the lucky category, but about half of our neighbors weren't so fortunate.

A large number of neighborhood children, therefore, were left home alone. Anyone older than fifteen had already been sent down to work in the countryside. Children over twelve, especially girls, took charge of raising their siblings. Children were divided into two factions, based on how their parents were treated. Those who came from "good" families despised those who came from "bad" ones, and refused to associate with them. They called us names, and threw stones at us.

With no school to attend and desperate for food, children started to raise farm animals in the very limited space that was available. Chicken was a common choice, for it was a source of eggs and meat. We raised a few hens and a couple of roosters.

Most of the eggs were carefully saved, and before we knew it, a new generation of chicks came into the world.

My favorite hen—we named her "Little Yellow"—became a proud new mother to a dozen cute chicks with bright yellow feathers. In order to distinguish our chicks from those raised by others, we dyed their heads red.

Little Yellow was a smart hen, but not smart enough to understand who her enemies were supposed to be. She befriended another hen who was owned by our next-door neighbor. Their chicks mingled with one another, and happily searched for worms and nuts as a group.

Our neighbor's child discovered this politically incorrect mixing, and resolved to separate the two mothers and their chicks. He threw stones at Little Yellow to drive her away. During the process, one of her chicks was stoned to death.

Witnessing this tragedy, I was furious. I rushed out and screamed. A layer of blood now bespangled the ink-dyed head, and though two tiny feet were still kicking, the young bird's life was already over. While I knew that my best hope of staying out of trouble was not to provoke the "privileged" children, I was absolutely furious, and my head was spinning with the impulse to extract revenge. An eye for an eye, after all. For the first time, I felt a great desire to take a life.

The next day, I waited until no one was watching the neighbor's hen and her chicks, and I went over and caught one of the chicks. The mother did not protest, since she was accustomed to having humans around.

The small chick sang happily in my hand. His light yellow feathers shined brightly under the sun. He shook his wings and tail cheerfully, giving me a gesture of welcome. And my heart melted. After a few minutes, the mother called out impatiently. I put the chick down and turned back. The little thing followed me at first, but was called back by the mother.

Why did people have to be enemies of one another? Why on earth did "class struggle" have to involve chickens? The political insanity was so pervasive that no one, even a small animal, could escape. I wanted no part of it.

STORY SIXTEEN: CALL IT A VICTORY

On April 1, 1969, the Chinese Communist Party held its Ninth Party Congress, during which the Party declared the "overall victory" of the Cultural Revolution. Seventy-five percent of the members of the Party Central Committee selected by the Eighth Congress in 1956 were gone. A few had died, but most had been purged. The number-two man, Liu Shaoqi, was in a special jail, dying from starvation and disease. He was left in bed alone, lying in his own urine and feces. Millions of people—most of the veteran Communist Party leaders, intellectuals, the "bad classes," and other designated "enemies of the people"—were either in prison, in detention centers or labor camps, or in exile in poor rural areas.

After purging his political rivals in this mass movement, Mao sent the military out to stop the civil war, but war continued in many parts of the country. More military forces were sent out, accordingly. More people were killed, detained, and arrested. A new round of terror was launched, and Mao and his cohorts called it victory. In 1969, with millions of people persecuted, the Cultural Revolution was declared a "total" victory. The victory was marked by routine mass public executions from the fall of 1968 to the end of 1970.

On a cold winter day in 1968, I came face to face with people who were about to be executed. A hundred thousand residents of the city were assembled by the military in several public squares. A sentencing rally was held in the Yuexiu Arena. From the beginning of the Cultural Revolution, this famous sports arena had been used as the principal venue for political rallies. A few times a month, the condemned were put on stage and forced to face an angry mob. They would be compelled to wear heavy signs around their necks with their names and ostensible crimes written on them. Since the signs had to be big enough to be visible to people in the back rows, they usually weighed thirty to fifty pounds. If the victims were important enough, they might also be denounced on the same spot, and paraded around and humiliated.

At this rally, the military rulers announced the sentences of dozens of people. Those sentenced were forced onto this stage. If a big red cross appeared over their names on the signs they bore around their necks, it meant they had been sentenced to death. After the rally, they would be paraded around for a couple of hours and then executed.

I was among the thousands who stood along the street, watching the trucks with the doomed people moving slowly, an unmistakable display of the power and brutality of the regime.

A young man with old-fashioned rimmed glasses was among the unfortunate. Two soldiers behind him were holding his head down, depriving him of his last chance to see the city and the people. Blood was dripping from his mouth, adding more red to the red cross over his name.

Even at a height of only four and a half feet, I got a glimpse of the condemned man's face. It was ashen pale, with all the color concentrated in the fresh blood stain on the sign he was bearing, on which the word "counterrevolutionary" had been written. He looked about twenty, certainly no more than twenty-five. I could not even begin to imagine the agony that young man was going through. To me, the scene itself was unbearable.

That face will remain with me forever, a perennial reminder of the despicable evil of Maoism.

Much later, when the Cultural Revolution ended, official records revealed that the military or the police routinely cut out the tongues of the victims before execution in order to prevent them from speaking or shouting. So there was no shouting from the condemned, only from the crowd. Led by the Party activists among them, they hurled insults at those poor people who were about to meet a violent death.

Yet for my part, I could not hear anything. To me, it was deadly silent. The entire society. The whole of China. There were no dissenting voices among this deafening noise. There was no real emotion in it except fear. Every participant put on the same performance, and was "heated in a cool way," to borrow de Tocqueville's expression regarding the French Terror.

The military controlled our city with an iron fist. As if sending so many adults away was not enough, in the winter of 1969 it ordered all middle school–aged students to be sent to rural areas to build new schools far from the city with their young hands. This was considered the best possible type of education. Since the Cultural Revolution had essentially destroyed the economy, there were few job openings in urban areas anyway, and all the colleges were closed. All except a handful of young people would have to be sent to work in rural areas anyway. Why not start early?

That was also the year in which China and the Soviet Union experienced a few border incidents. Gunshots were fired, and a few soldiers were killed. It gave the military more legitimacy in increasing its control over civilians. A war between China and the Soviet Revisionists would be launched very soon, claimed the military. By dispersing people away from the cities, the burden of defense would be minimized.

No transportation was provided to the students for this journey. Schools, which were reassembled hastily after having been closed since 1966, organized the students for a long march.

For two full days, I trudged with 180 other thirteen- to fifteen-year-olds to a village fifty miles away. We carried our own luggage. We learned how to bind everything together in military-style backpacks—wrapping a small comforter and all our other belongings with a sheet made of straw. After a few hours' walk, however, even the paltry belongings we had brought along became unbearably heavy. A cold winter rain dramatically increased the difficulty. Soaked with water, the straw sheet seemed to weigh a hundred pounds. We saw other schools marching on the same road, and suddenly, my eyes caught sight of a strange image: a large, round, black object with two feet walking a hundred feet in front of me. Curiosity prompted me to catch up with the object. When I approached it, I realized that it was a male student—fourteen years old, perhaps—carrying a big iron cooking wok on his back. It was the type used in the military for cooking and must have weighed at least twenty-five pounds. Poor guy! But he seemed not to be suffering, but rather to be proud of looking so masculine.

When we finally reached the mountainous village, we thought we had come to the end of the known universe. We were immediately divided into small teams, lead by a group of villagers who had been appointed to guide us in the construction of houses and classrooms.

Working ten to twelve hours a day in the fields or on construction projects was hard work, but I did not mind it. It was the solitude that was unbearable. I could find no books to read there. My peers were not very interesting. For children who were entering adolescence, the whole situation was terribly confusing. There was little fun in our lives, and there was not much of a future in sight.

Terror, of course, did not extend only to the cities. It also found its way to this poor, remote area. In February 1970, a new political campaign called the "One Attack and Three Antis" campaign was launched. If the Terror of 1966 to 1969 focused mainly on "old" class enemies, namely those who had some association with the pre-Communist days, this new campaign targeted the "newborn counterrevolutionaries," namely those who had voiced dissent against the Party, and particularly against Mao, in recent years. Over the previous four years, killings had mostly been conducted by mass organizations such as the Red Guards. In 1970, however, the sentences were handed down by the legal system. In order to speed up the persecution, county-level governments were given the power to authorize death sentences.

People were arrested with very little cause, such as having stained Mao's portrait by accident. Most were sentenced quickly. Colleagues affiliated with the same work unit as the accused were normally assembled by the authorities and asked to denounce the person. By the end of the session, someone—usually appointed by the authorities—would yell:

"The revolutionary masses demand that this counterrevolutionary be sentenced to death!"

And no one dared object. Many death sentences were determined in this way, and followed immediately by execution.

A friend of mine, a college student at the time, was arrested for making a few jokes in private gatherings. He was sentenced to death in such a fashion. Luckily for him, someone in authority happened to know his father, and his sentence was commuted to life imprisonment. His schoolmates, who were present at those same gatherings, were not so lucky. They were executed; my friend only spent ten years in jail.

We were allowed to take a day off once in a while to go to the county bazaar, which was held every ten days. Public sentencing rallies were organized on bazaar days and they were followed by public executions. Several times, we were asked by the local authorities to witness the event.

The chosen execution site was on the river bank, not far from a bridge. People could see the entire process clearly from the banks or the bridge, but would not be able either to see the faces of the victims or to hear what they had to say.

On one particular day, two people were scheduled for execution. My fellow students and I were asked to stand on the bridge. Two hundred feet away, members of the local militia dragged two guys to the execution site. They were both in their twenties or thirties; it was hard to tell. A long wooden plank—about five or six feet in length—was tightened onto each one's back. On it was written the victim's name, marked with a big, red cross.

"These are thieves. They stole something from the people's commune," I heard someone with a local accent mutter in the back row. The militia pushed the two guys into a kneeling position. Then someone wearing a military uniform took a pistol and quickly shot both victims in the back of their heads. They fell instantly.

The sound of the pistol was unexpectedly muted. The viewers quickly dispersed. No one said anything, as if the killings were simply part of the normal ritual. Since that time, I have often thought that had I been ten years older during that time period, I would surely have suffered the same fate as many of the executed. Even at that age—thirteen—I already harbored thoughts that, if expressed, would be punishable by death.

Even in this remote village, no one was able to escape the brutality of the Party. Every word uttered, every sign drawn, and every gesture made would be interpreted by an army of Party activists. And they were everywhere, in all age groups and organizations. The Party, with its millions of its activists, penetrated deeply into the society.

All the youngsters in our group were working ten to twelve hours a day building houses for the new school compound. We were also perpetually hungry, since food supplies in rural areas were much more sparse than in the city. One day, someone found a few words scratched under a window in our new classroom.

"Shaoqi, good."

Shaoqi was Liu Shaoqi, the former president. He had died in prison the previous year.

Who dared write such a thing? Didn't he know it was more than enough to send him directly to prison?

The handwriting seemed immature. The authorities decided that it must have been done by one of the youngsters from the city, since poor rural children would not express such a "reactionary feeling." They started to examine the family backgrounds of all the students, and quickly zeroed in on one.

She was my friend Huang. One year older than I, she came from a formerly rich family. Her father was a famous railway engineer. Both of her parents were in labor camps at the time. She seemed like someone who would miss Liu Shaoqi, the authorities concluded.

This fifteen-year-old girl was immediately put under detention. The authorities assembled a special case team, consisting of a few adults and three or four student activists who had solid family backgrounds. The team interrogated Huang for more than ten hours until she admitted the crime.

During the next few days, Huang was forced to stand in front of all the students, confessing her crime and denouncing herself. One after another, the student activists, with prepared scripts in hand, went on to denounce her. From then on, she became damaged goods. No one dared be her friend anymore.

Before I fully comprehended what was happening to Huang, I was summoned to the classroom. The day was April 22, 1970, when the loudspeaker outside was broadcasting an editorial from the *People's Daily* celebrating Lenin's one hundredth birthday. Many of my classmates—about fifty or sixty—were already there. I was asked to stand in front of the entire class, facing the others.

I obeyed, with a very uneasy feeling. I had seen such struggle sessions way too many times before.

A student activist took out a script and started reading. It detailed a conversation I had had with another student during which I complained about the lack of books. I had also said that I wished I could have some music with me. My family owned a phonograph, and I was thinking of taking it with me when I grew up.

"Capitalist lifestyle!"

"Little revisionist!"

"Little bad element!" my inquisitors declared.

Student activists came up to me, one after another. For an entire hour, I listened to all the epithets they hurled at me, and was completely devastated. I did not regret what I had said; it had, in reality, been only a small part of what I was really thinking. But I regretted having talked to anyone. I swore I would never again disclose any thoughts, even the most seemingly innocent ones, to anyone.

It was two months before my fourteenth birthday.

STORY SEVENTEEN: MY SECRET GARDEN

On a hot summer day in 1999, I held a party in the backyard of my home in northern Virginia. My brother James, a very established electrical engineer, was visiting from China. My friend Kelu Chao, program director of the Voice of America, was among the guests.

When I introduced Kelu to James, he was thrilled.

"I know you! I heard your voice years ago! I still remember it!"

Kelu had been a veteran radio broadcaster for VOA since the mid-1970s. Her signature voice once opened a secret window for us in China, and brought us much joy.

In 1971, James, then thirteen, began his career as an engineer. Father, released after two years of detention, encouraged James to explore the world of radio technology, and gave him a small sum to start him off. Using ancient instructions, James constructed a crystal shortwave radio. With a pair of headphones, he was able to pick up signals from foreign radio stations being broadcast into China, principally the Voice of America. He shared his secret with me.

It was difficult to receive the signal during the day, due to government jamming. By midnight, though, the voices were sometimes clear.

After a short rendition of Yankee Doodle, the announcer came on:

"This is the Voice of America. I am so-and-so. Let's begin with the news."

The voices were so fresh, so personal and so pleasant compared to the shrill, piercing sound of Chinese government broadcasters!

The programs we loved most included the news, the music, and the English class. Due to constant jamming, the broadcast was never stable for more than a few minutes. But those minutes were treasures in our lives. We learned about American opinions of Nixon's historic visit to China, Mao's illness, Watergate, and Nixon's resignation, among many other things. We also picked up some English. Only the jamming prevented us from learning more.

As I write, thirty-five years later, about this early English learning experience, I am still amazed by it. Speaking a foreign language proved to be so refreshing and so liberating to our minds. During those years, when people talked about "self" in Chinese, they were taught to speak collectively: "we hope," "we want," and "we think." That is, unless they were talking negatively about themselves, at which point it became "I made a mistake" or "I did not follow the chairman's teaching." Anyone who used the first person too often was accused of being selfish. In English, I could speak about what "I" wanted, and what "I" hoped. It was a guiltless "I," an "I" that had more or less been expelled from the Chinese language in that era and that did not make a comeback until the 1980s.

We also picked up signals from Radio Moscow. It sounded a lot like Chinese government radio, except that it constantly attacked the Chinese Communist Party. Its signature sign-in was, "This is Radio Peace and Progress. We are here in Moscow." It had some fantastic Russian music, though. The most-jammed signals were from Taiwan, and the least-jammed was Radio

Pyongyang. It also played Russian music from time to time, which made Radio Pyongyang sometimes sound heavenly.

The radios became our secret garden. James and I loved them. Years later, this experience played a role in my decision to give up a career in academia and join Radio Free Asia.

I must say that it was courageous for Father to allow his son to explore this activity. Those were years during which the most innocent acts could readily be interpreted as politically subversive, and this, if discovered, would be considered anything but innocent. Those interested in radio technology were often accused of "secretly listening to enemy propaganda," a criminal offense punishable by a long prison sentence. Yet many people took the risk in order to satisfy their irrepressible desire for information and truth.

In 1971, James began his career as one of China's best communications engineers. I had already started mine as an unrepentant political dissident, for I treasured books, and the independent thinking they induced, more than anything—not just *any* books, but books that conveyed beauty and inspired thinking.

At the time, China had one monopoly chain bookstore, the Xinhua Bookstore. If you walked into any one of them, you'd see more than half of the shelves occupied by Mao's books—four volumes of his selected works and the notorious Little Red Book of his quotations. There might be ten or twenty other books available, all of them poorly written works of government propaganda.

Even the best-trained writers could not write government propaganda that was enjoyable to read. There was only a limited number of words, expressions, and emotions that were considered acceptable for this type of writing. Almost all such works began and ended with something like this:

"Following Great Leader Chairman Mao's teachings, our Party ..." or, "We condemn so-and-so, who has proven to be opposed to Mao Zedong's thought ..." An entire generation grew up with that kind of drivel in all their basic educational materials. Classical Chinese literature, on the other hand, was among the richest and the most beautiful in human history. The written characters have lasted for five thousand years. The language of Confucius, of Tang Dynasty poems and Song Dynasty lyrics, was still alive and used in our daily life. I adored the ancient authors and their works. I memorized many of them, and can still recite them by heart.

I also loved European literature. Beginning in the late nineteenth century, much Western literature was translated into Chinese, especially French and Russian novels. I wasn't so thrilled by the French, except for Victor Hugo, but I loved the Russian authors. Perhaps it was their profound sadness and deep sense of humanity that moved me so greatly.

My parents did not approve of my hobby. In fact, all the books I loved were banned. While the Red Guards were burning books taken from the libraries and houses they ransacked, the government closed down all the libraries and banned all books published before the Cultural Revolution, except for Mao's books, of course. Adults and children alike were urged to monitor other people and their households to discover and report anyone who possessed "bad" books.

Moved either by a natural instinct to preserve our common heritage or perhaps just out of basic human decency, many families hid, rather than destroyed, their books. My parents kept hundreds of their academic books, but locked them up to prevent us reading them. Therefore, going through our parents' belongings and stealing books became a common game among adolescents. The children quietly circulated the books among themselves. A quid pro quo system was established under which everyone became both a lender and a borrower. The more books one could find to lend out, the more favors others would return. Sometimes a book was so popular that each borrower was given only a few hours to read it. The most treasured books were sometimes even hand-copied and then circulated. I participated in several such projects, including producing a copy of Pushkin's poetry by hand.

Some parents tolerated or even quietly encouraged these activities. Others—including, of course, my mother—adhered more closely to the Party line. The more rigid parents would go through their children's belongings, confiscating all unsuitable objects. So kids from those families were forced to develop more thorough methods of concealing their books.

One day in 1970, a girl from my neighborhood and I were reading a book together. It was a book about the archeological history of Chinese Turkestan, which we called Xinjiang. It was a very well-written book with many pictures, published for high school students in the 1950s. I borrowed it from a kid in our neighborhood who had taken it from his parents' collection, and I was allowed to have it for only a few hours. I knew that my mother, who had already been released from the detention center and was now home from time to time, would not approve of the book. So I went to another girl's apartment and read it together with her.

The book was extremely interesting. We absorbed it like dry sponges, and were mesmerized by the illustrations in it. Suddenly, her mother, a high school physics teacher, appeared from out of nowhere. When she spotted the book in our hands, she immediately seized it.

"What kind of trash you are reading?" She seemed very angry. We didn't dare utter a word in our defense. She continued, "This is a revisionist book. It poisons your mind. I am taking it away!"

Oh, my book, my book! My kingdom for that book! I moaned to myself. But I had no kingdom to offer. The book was gone forever, confiscated by someone who was supposed to be a teacher. I don't remember how I compensated the book owner for the loss of property, thought I'm sure we worked it out somehow. But nowadays, when I close my eyes and think of that incident, I can still taste the feelings of panic and desperation.

Not much reading was allowed, and not much writing was taught. All writing had to follow a certain pattern which was modeled after government propaganda, and which was, of course, deadly dull.

One day in 1971, I came back from the village and saw a piece of paper under the glass that covered my father's desk. It was written by James. It read:

"The Supreme Instruction from Chairman Mao: We must struggle against selfishness and criticize revisionism. I stole and ate meat. Why did I make such a mistake? It was because I did not study Chairman Mao's works hard enough. From now on, I will study hard and correct my misbehavior."

My brother was forced to write this ridiculous self-criticism for the crime of taking a small piece of meat from the family kitchen. He was, at the time, a thirteen-year-old boy who never had enough to eat.

Besides this kind of writing—criticizing oneself or someone else, or praising Mao and the Party—no other writing was allowed unless the writer was bound and determined to get him or herself into very deep trouble.

Even personal diaries were often written as if someone were watching. Several of the books still available in bookstores were diaries of model soldiers who had died in the line of duty. After their death, their diaries were published. These journals were filled with their worshipful thoughts about Mao, and recorded how they followed Mao's instructions every minute of their lives. Once those diaries were published, the schools encouraged all students to write diaries, and to read them aloud in front of their classes. Millions of youngsters wrote this rubbish every day, faking their thoughts and sometimes even making up activities of whole cloth. They dreamed that their diaries might someday be added to the short list of volumes available in the bookstores. Diaries were no longer private.

Meanwhile, anyone who wrote down his or her true thoughts and feelings was taking a big risk. Genuine, private, human feelings always include doubts and dissatisfaction with those who exercise power or control over their lives. Diaries were routinely taken when houses were ransacked, at work, or by accident. Sometimes family members who discovered diaries with "bad" thoughts might actually hand them over to the authorities. Thus thousands or tens of thousands of people were sent to jail simply because they spoke their minds in the privacy of their own diaries.

I kept a diary briefly when I was eleven. Being me, I recorded some of my doubts about my parents and their methods of controlling us. Mother, who routinely searched my belongings, eventually found it. It was not a very pleasant scene, my parents summoning me and showering me with curses.

But I could not help myself. I kept writing down my thoughts. And once or twice a week, I would take all my writings, tear them apart, and bury them in a corner of our courtyard, a shameless imitation of a young girl in the classic Chinese novel *The Dream of the Red Chamber*, who collected, mourned, and buried the fallen flowers. I didn't really need the paper copies. My thoughts were buried anyhow—not only in the ground, but also deep in my mind.

STORY EIGHTEEN: I AM NOT WHAT I AM

The situation had improved considerably by 1972, the year Nixon came to China and I got my first job.

The brutality of the Cultural Revolution had reached its peak in 1970, when massive numbers of people were detained, imprisoned, or executed. This intense persecution terrorized the entire population. It also, paradoxically, embittered even some of the most zealous Communist believers. What was the point of a revolution when the results included total tyranny over people's minds and extreme economic hardship? The Maoist revolution devoured everyone, parents and children alike. Former Red Guards and rebels were all sent down to do hard labor in the countryside; Communist cadres were deprived of power and privileges; and the "bad classes" were perpetual victims. Ultimately, nobody was a winner, not even the tyrant himself. Mao became old, sick, and totally isolated. He had successfully gotten rid of all his friends and comrades, whom he suspected to be his rivals. Now he had to endure loneliness and betrayal.

When this victimization took a new turn in 1971, disillusion became widespread. On September 13, Marshal Lin Biao, the defense minister who was Mao's appointed successor, fled the country after a failed coup and attempt to assassinate Mao. On his way to the Soviet Union, his plane crashed in Mongolia—at least that was the official version.

No one was more radical than Lin. In 1964, he had launched the Mao cult within the military, a cult that later spread throughout the society. He was always at Mao's side when the Great Helmsman reviewed his Red Guards on parade. He was the incarnation of the militarization of the nation in 1968. He always talked about Mao as if Mao were the only true God.

And now he was dead after a failed attempt to assassinate Mao. What an irony. Suddenly, the tension broke. People began to whisper to one another about the "mistakes" of the Cultural Revolution. Their fear of, and respect for, the military declined palpably.

Many parents began to refuse to send their children to the countryside. Usually, it was working class parents who did so. Perhaps it was because they had more common sense than the intellectuals and cadres, or perhaps they just had less to lose.

After Lin's death, purged officials started to return to their previous government positions. My parents were also released from their detention centers, and they came back to reclaim their teaching jobs. Middle schools reopened, although students were still required to work in the countryside for two or three months a year. Things seemed, gradually, to return to normalcy, whatever that meant under Communism.

As a result, some urban jobs opened up. And so when I reached sixteen, the government assigned me a job in a candy factory. It was a factory located in a working class neighborhood in the center of Guangzhou. A large coal furnace burned in it day and night, and its huge chimney spread black coal dust everywhere within a radius of a hundred yards.

Apart from that, the factory did not look like an industrial facility at all. The building actually looked more residential, with a six-foot-wide door as its major entrance. The structure had three levels, each about ten thousand square feet in area. Seven hundred workers worked three shifts there. Three hundred young workers between the ages of sixteen and nineteen were added that year. I was one of them.

I was assigned to work the candy-shaping machines. My team changed shifts every week: first the day shift, from 7 a.m. to 3:30 p.m., then the evening shift, from 3:30 p.m. to 12:00 midnight, and finally the night shift, from midnight to 7 a.m.

The veteran workers, mostly middle-aged women, took us in warmly. They told us the night shift was a good deal. It had fewer hours, and the factory provided a free meal. But the job wasn't easy. Every fifteen minutes, I had to carry a sixty-pound piece of raw, half-melting candy across a fifty-foot hallway, dodging several machines along the way, and put the material into the shaping machine.

These were very old machines, some dating from the 1930s, and they broke down constantly. I quickly learned how to repair them, since they were rather simple mechanisms. But with old machines like these, accidents happened all the time. I lost half a finger during a night shift while I was repairing a machine that suddenly started up. Almost all machine operators were injured at one point or another; no one paid much attention.

In fact, the party leaders told all the young workers that we were extremely lucky to have a job. And we knew it was true. "You must thank Chairman Mao and the Party!" said the factory's Party leaders. This was supposed to be our lifetime employment. The only path leading beyond the current position involved becoming a very good Party activist; this was how promotions could be won.

Besides the average eight-hour shift and six-day workweek, workers were also required to attend three ninety-minute political sessions each week. Most were little more than newspaper-reading sessions, since there was not much else that could be said, especially in politics. The Party leaders laid down the rules for these sessions: no napping, no chatting, no knitting (a very popular activity among female workers), and no reading—not even the same newspaper that was being read aloud. Violators would have to pay fines: money would be taken from their pay.

I refused to believe that this job would be my final lot in life. At the age of sixteen, a year seemed an extremely long time. Having a dull job, having no opportunity, and having no future were very difficult concepts for any sixteen-year-old to swallow. So I tried not to think of my future, and instead buried myself deeply in books. I wrote as often as I read—articles, poems, notes, etc., and continued to destroy whatever I put down on paper. I was convinced that the Maoist version of Communism was possibly the worst system in the world. I had no interest in being a Party activist in any way. Had I tried, I would not have succeeded anyway. If I had known better, I would have sought out other like-minded young people in the workplace. But they were in hiding, just as I was.

One day in 1974, a fellow worker—a nineteen-year-old man—was arrested by the police. After a few weeks, the factory held a rally. Even the night shifters were ordered to attend. Mei, the young man was brought to the stage in handcuffs by two policemen. His head was shaved bald. His face was snow white. He twisted his body violently, as if this could set him free. He looked much younger than his age, almost like a kid.

The factory party leader announced Mei's crime. He had an uncle who had fled to Taiwan with the Nationalist government in 1949. Mei had listened to a Taiwan radio broadcast and sent a letter via the address provided by the station. In that letter, addressed to his uncle, he complained about the terrible life on the mainland. "Not much to eat, not much to read, and not much to see," he said in the letter. He had asked if his uncle could find a way to send him some books.

Listening to enemy radio and contacting the enemies—these were pieces of evidence cited to demonstrate that he had volunteered to be an enemy agent. One of the policemen read his sentence out loud. Mei would be jailed for the next eight years. (He actually stayed in prison for only four years. He was released in 1978, after Mao's death, when many political prisoners gained their freedom.)

Another young man was also arrested in the same year, but for different reasons. Li was on my work team, and he had been my partner at work from time to time. He was an extremely shy guy who would not talk to the young women at work unless it was absolutely necessary. His fellow workers often wondered if there was something wrong with him.

One day, he failed to show up at work, and the next day we heard that he had been arrested. On his way back from an evening shift, he had attacked a young woman and tried to rape her, but she managed to escape and went to the police. When the police asked her to describe the perpetrator, she replied that she had not gotten a good look at him, but remembered that the man had smelled of candy. The police checked the residents in the nearby neighborhood, and quickly zeroed in on him. The young man was sentenced to ten years.

For the hormone-driven young men and women in the factory, sex was the most taboo of subjects. Neither schools nor workplaces ever provided any sex education to young people. Nor were any books on the subject available. Even banned books published before the Cultural Revolution were completely sanitized. Young people therefore had to rely on rumor and whispers to learn whatever they could.

Premarital sex was absolutely forbidden, but of course many people engaged in it anyway. In the mid-seventies, when the government first began serious efforts to control population growth, it changed the official ages for marriage. Although legally the ages were eighteen for females and twenty for males, an executive order from the Guangzhou municipal government denied marriage licenses to any female under twenty-four and any male under twenty-seven, unless they had special permission.

As a consequence, premarital sex and unwanted pregnancy were widespread.

That afternoon, after we finished a day shift, the entire work team—about fifteen people—gathered for our regular political session. Instead of meeting in the regular corner, however, we were summoned to a private room, one typically used for meetings among Party members and the factory leaders. A Party activist put a stool in the middle of the room after we all sat down, and ordered a twenty-one-year-old girl on our team to sit on it. I immediately recalled the session convened to criticize me a few years before, and realized what was about to happen. This girl was in trouble.

The Party activist hosted the meeting. She announced that so-and-so had made a very bad mistake, and that she would confess all to her fellow workers. Then, head bowed low, the girl started to read from a written confession. She said she had made a terrible mistake under the influences of capitalist thinking, and had had an "incorrect" relationship with a man in another factory. She was pregnant. She begged for everyone's forgiveness, and asked for a "new opportunity to be a new person." Publicly humiliated, she cried bitterly as she read.

I was shocked, because she was normally a very quiet and passive girl. The veteran workers—many of them housewives drafted to the workforce in 1958—were a lot more sympathetic than the Party leaders. When she finished, the forewoman—not a Party member—said assertively, "We are all tired after this long shift. Let's go home."

She said it with such authority that the Party activist did not dare protest. She was a highly respected worker with more than thirty years' experience.

All women—married or not—who wanted to terminate pregnancy had to show the hospitals written approval from their work units, or else the doctors would not perform abortions. With the approval of our unit, the girl on our team had one, and she married the same man three years later when she reached the age of twenty-four.

Another frequently discussed subject among young people was how to flee to Hong Kong. The fact that this occurred from time to time was an open secret in Guangdong Province, which abuts Hong Kong geographically, and which shares a dialect with the then-British crown colony. Although there were always people who tried to flee to Hong Kong, the two biggest waves of refugees occurred between 1959 and 1962 during the Great Famine, and between 1970 and 1980. The first wave consisted mainly of hungry peasants from the border regions. The second involved mostly desperate youth who had been sent to work in rural areas or factories where they saw no future for themselves.

Maps of sea and land paths to Hong Kong, nicknamed "chessboards," were quietly circulated among young people. Every day after our shift, a few young people, mostly male, would pick up their swimming suits and say to each other, "Let's go and practice!"

In those days, the Pearl River was filled with young people determined to flee to Hong Kong. Close to the sea, the river had a strong tide, and thus swimming in it was not unlike swimming in the sea. In 1974, therefore, the Guangzhou police banned swimming in the river, but the ban did not stop the most determined swimmers. Each afternoon, the police would send out a few speed boats and detain them. Before long, the police were overwhelmed.

The border patrol was overwhelmed, too. At the beginning of the 1970s, those who were caught on their way to Hong Kong might be given jail sentences. By the mid-1970s, when hundreds of people were caught each day, the penitentiary system lost its ability to process them. After all, what more could the government do to already desperate people?

Periodically, young men disappeared from work. Some succeeded in fleeing and settled in Hong Kong. Some were sent back after a few days. Their heads were shaved from having endured a few days of detention, which was the punishment. They did not seem to care at all. Instead, they wore their bald heads like badges of honor.

Those kinds of activities did not interest me much. I was preoccupied by something else. I had finally found a group of like-minded friends.

STORY NINETEEN: REBEL WITH A CAUSE

One day in April 1974, I finished my night shift at the factory and rode home on my bicycle. While passing one of the busiest intersections in downtown Guangzhou, I noticed a large crowd gathering. People were standing in front of several posters painted, in typical Cultural Revolution style, with big, black characters, and reading intently.

One particular poster—entitled *Whither Guangdong?*—attracted great attention.

In 1967, a similar poster entitled *Whither China?* had instigated national excitement. The poster was written by a sixteen-year-old middle school student named Yang Xiguang. On it, Yang criticized Premier Zhou Enlai, who was the symbol of political moderation at the time, and urged a more extreme direction for the Cultural Revolution. He named his own brand of thinking "ultra-leftism." Most similar attacks against Party leaders were either orchestrated or sanctioned from the very top. For instance, the rebel leader at Qinghua University, Kuai Dafu, received direct instructions from one of Mao's most trusted cohorts, Kang Sheng, before he turned China's then-President Liu Shaoqi into a target. Unlike Kuai, however, Yang had neither instruction nor sanction from the top. He was quickly arrested and put in jail for the next ten years. The empire of Mao persecuted free thinkers indiscriminately, whether they were from the right or from the left.

Yang, however, had set a precedent for public discussion of the direction of the nation, which was the cause of the excitement. In other words, the title of his article was at least as important as its content, if not more so.

So when an article entitled *Whither Guangdong?* appeared on a public bulletin board, people remembered the other article and became excited. The author signed his name Li Yizhe.

1974 was a strange year. The Cultural Revolution had finally run totally out of steam, especially after Lin Biao's death. For his part, though, Mao, the "continuous revolutionary," tried to rejuvenate it early that year by launching a "Criticize Confucius and Lin Biao" campaign.

I loved Confucius and his teachings. I could recite almost every line of his works by heart. Confucianism had provided the Chinese with a solid national value system. It struck a balance between reason and passion, and promoted humility and tolerance.

Confucianism, whose main theme was one of centrism and conservatism, was a favorite target of the radicals in the twentieth century. Such radicalism promoted extremism and nurtured Communism. The radicals argued that Confucianism, the ideology of feudalism, was not compatible with modernity, and often blamed it for blocking China's path to new greatness. However, the more I understood how history progressed, the more I came to appreciate Confucianism.

Of course, it was easy to criticize a doctrine that was two and half millennia old for backwardness. It did, indeed, discriminate against women, and it emphasized loyalty over many other virtues. But it was no more backward than other ancient documents—the Bible, for instance. The best of the teachings of our ancestors were flexible enough to be updated with time, but solid in their core values. They reflected wisdom and the inner strength that permitted Chinese civilization to survive, grow, and evolve.

Now Mao wanted to link Confucianism with his late, estranged deputy, Lin Biao. There was no logic in it, and everyone could see this. But Mao also urged people to "follow the great tradition of the Cultural Revolution." That is, Mao encouraged people to express their opinions through "big-character posters." And like him, the authorities often believed they could manipulate these opinions and direct them to target whoever fell out of their favor. By this time, however, most people understood what was in their self interest much better than before. Instead of following Mao's instructions, many saw in the posters an opportunity to express their own grievances publicly. When the "big-character posters" appeared on the streets in 1974, a large percentage of them took an entirely different direction, and criticized the brutality of the extremely repressive years between 1968 and 1971, when the military had been under Lin Biao's leadership.

"*Whither Guangdong?*" was an article that led the charge. It attributed the brutality, the civil war, the economic disaster, and the misery of the early years to the "ultra-leftist line" of Lin Biao. It called for exoneration of the persecuted and the restoration of a reasonable legal system.

What it said was no more than common sense. Yet common sense was exactly what China had lacked during those crazy years. The article therefore immediately attracted thousands of readers. Hundreds of small notes supporting the author were fastened next to the poster. Apart from offering the unshakable logic of common sense, the article was also very well written: challenging, but not argumentative; eloquent, but not trite.

I had been secretly recording my own views on political philosophy for a while. A Harvard education, of course, was entirely out of the scope of my dreams at that time. I simply wrote for my own satisfaction and sanity. I began to favor history and theory books over novels, plowing through Marx and Engels and whatever other books on political theory I could get my hands on. I was particularly interested in reading the footnotes in the Marxist books, since they were full of references not otherwise taught in China—ancient Western mythology, Greek and Roman history, eighteenth- and nineteenth-century European history, etc. I felt like a plant in a desert, sinking roots into the most inaccessible of places in order to absorb some water. I hand-copied many books, sometimes with friends, sometimes alone, including an old translation of Friedrich Hayek's *The Road to Serfdom*. Hand-copying banned books had become one of the favorite activities of knowledge-thirsty young people like me.

As I read it, I immediately recognized the writing style of "*Whither Guangdong*?" I knew that the author must be a kindred spirit—we loved the same books and shared the same historical perspective and political ideas, except that the author was much more mature and better educated than I was. At the time, I had not yet reached my eighteenth birthday.

The feeling of excitement almost paralyzed me. Finally I had identified a comrade-in-arms and a possible teacher! But how could I find him?

I kept going to that intersection day after day, looking for a clue. Every few weeks, the author, Li Yizhe, posted a new article with more thoughts on the disaster of the Cultural Revolution (referring to it as the "Lin Biao system," in keeping with the Party campaign), on democracy (under the name of the ruthlessness of "mass democracy" promoted by Mao), and on the rule of law (under the name of the "socialist legal system"). I became a most faithful reader. I posted many small notes there in the middle of the night, when I was returning home from my evening shift or on my way to my night shift. I noticed that even in the wee small hours there were readers, and there were easy-to-spot plainclothes policemen as well.

"This person is courageous! He has spoken for all of us!" many readers commented in their notes.

Never before had an author criticized Communist rule so courageously, thoroughly, and convincingly. Not in my brief lifetime, anyway. People predicted that he would be arrested before long, yet he kept posting. In November 1974, he posted a landmark article entitled *On Socialist Democracy and the Legal System*. It summarized all the ideas in the previous posters. It called for true democracy and a legal system. It was eye-opening for many people.

The summer and fall of 1974 was a very unusual period. For the first time, Mao's mobilization tactics did not work. Although government media made a great deal of noise, work units held rallies, and Party leaders encouraged people to post articles, few people were participating with any enthusiasm. Rather, the further exposure of Lin Biao's "crimes"—from his son's womanizing to his wife's extramarital affairs—made Mao and the Cultural Revolution seem like bad and cruel jokes.

Mass-movement tactics, which had victimized millions since the Communist takeover in 1949, also backfired. Big-character posters that were organized by the Party were hardly read, but those criticizing the Cultural Revolution drew people in like bees to honey.

Both the ideas and the language in posters like *Whither Guangdong?* were clearly punishable. Yet local governments delayed their crackdowns. Many, if not the majority, of local leaders had themselves been victimized in the previous years, and had come back to power only after Lin Biao's death. They were sympathetic to many of the rebellious posters. Nor did they want to experience another Cultural Revolution and expose themselves to the criticism that they had suppressed the masses.

The then–Party secretary of Guangdong Province, Zhao Ziyang, was among such government officials. Zhao, later premier and general secretary of the Communist Party in the 1980s, had joined the Communists in the 1930s. It was widely reported that his father, a landlord, had been executed or persecuted to death by Zhao's comrades in the late 1940s during the land reform program. An idealistic and humane man, he allowed the peasants in his district to have a little more freedom in planting their own land during the Great Leap Forward, and prevented a lot of deaths. In 1966, Zhao became the primary target in the province, attacked first by the Red Guards and then by the rebels. He was publicly humiliated and tortured. At many public rallies, he had to wear a huge dunce cap and carry a heavy sign that read "the major capitalist roader in the province." He was then placed in detention until 1972.

In 1974, Zhao was again put in charge of the Party in Guangdong. In the summer of 1975, the Party sent him to lead Sichuan, the most populous province in China, where he initiated seminal economic reforms. "Need to eat? Look for Ziyang!" was a ditty repeated often among peasants at the time.

A friend of mine worked for Zhao in Sichuan. He related a very telling story in which Zhao took a group of important Western visitors to see the streets of Chengdu, the capital of Sichuan. It was a rainy day. The interpreter apologized to the guests, as a true Chinese person would:

"Sorry. The weather is bad."

He dutifully translated the sentence back to Zhao. Unexpectedly, however, Zhao exploded:

"What do you mean bad weather? Tell them the weather is good. If it were sunny, they would see lots of beggars on the street."

The interpreter was frightened. If he translated what Zhao said, it would be in the official record. Zhao, and possibly the interpreter himself, would be accused of "damaging the image of the great motherland." Many people had been sent to prison for saying far less than that.

He hesitated. Zhao let it go, and did not insist on a translation. In those years, it was almost unthinkable for any Chinese, let alone a Party leader, to express dissatisfaction with the "great socialist achievements" so openly to foreigners. And Zhao was known to be a cautious person. The outburst must have reflected his true feelings on the failure of Communist economic policy.

Zhao became one of the leading lights in China's economic reform between 1978 and 1989. During the 1989 Tiananmen Square protest, however, he openly supported the demonstrators as the Party general secretary. He lost his position as a result, and died under house arrest sixteen years later.

Anyway, when the Li Yizhe posters, as they came to be called, began to appear, Zhao was in charge of Guangdong. When the party ideologues presented him with the Li articles and asked his approval to nip a potential rebellious movement in the bud, he calmly responded:

"The authors are young people. The posters are reactionary, but the authors don't yet quality as counterrevolutionaries." The subtlety in that remark could only be understood by people who came of age during that dangerous time. To be "counterrevolutionary" in and of itself was a crime punishable by prison. "Reactionary" was a description of seriously wrong thoughts or actions. "Counterrevolutionary" meant that the person belonged in jail; those who merely had "reactionary thoughts" might be "saved" by "education."

History would show that Zhao shared many of those "reactionary" thoughts. He was trying to save the authors from the most severe punishment. And, indeed, the authors—by that time I had already figured out that there was more than one and was myself deeply involved in the group—were thus not arrested until much later.

About two months after I read the first poster, the authors posted a note on the wall:

"We intend to print our posters for the people. We need a donation of plain paper. If you are willing to do so, bring the paper to Li Zhengtian at the dormitory of the Guangdong Art College."

I couldn't believe my luck. Immediately, I spent what little money I had saved and bought a large stack of paper. Carrying my contribution, I knocked at the door of Li Zhengtian's seventy-square-foot room. And that was how I met Li Zhengtian, the "Li" of Li Yizhe.

Li was a very short man, five-foot-two, perhaps, and very skinny. He wore a pair of dark-rimmed glasses, and a cap to cover his bald head. Trained as an oil painter, he was a college student and was very active during the Cultural Revolution. Having had a father who was once a Nationalist military officer, he naturally joined the rebels. He painted a great deal of rebel propaganda, I imagined.

Li invited me in, and we chatted. I told him about my family, my background, and some of the awful things that had happened to us during the previous years. He told me he had been in prison after the military took over in the fall of 1968, and that he had been released after four years. It was not an extraordinary story; it had happened to many people.

While we were chatting, a few more visitors arrived. Li introduced me to a couple of young men who seemed to be helping him with the printing. I offered my help. He accepted.

That was the beginning of my friendship and comradeship with a group of true rebels.

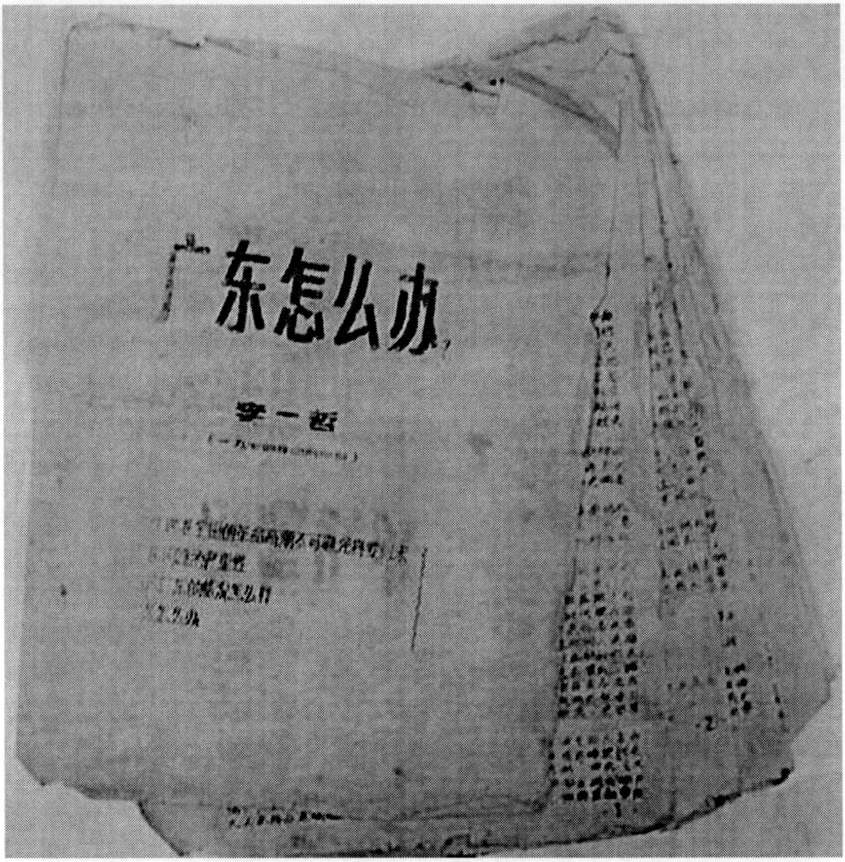

Figure 7. A mimeographed copy of *Whither Guangdong?*, which first appeared as a big character poster in Guangzhou in 1974. It was this essay that led me to join the Li Yizhe study group and launched my career as a dissident in China.

STORY TWENTY: FRIENDSHIP AND CAMARADERIE

I began my career as a political dissident by printing pamphlets, just as Benjamin Franklin, John Adams, and Thomas Paine did.

The printing process was in itself an interesting story. Although the Chinese invented movable type during the Song Dynasty hundreds of years before Gutenberg, they learned wax paper printing from the West.

In this era of computers and personal printers, I doubt many people remember wax paper printing. It is a simple but effective technology—a primitive form of the mimeograph. Using an iron tool, one carefully stencils words onto a piece of wax paper. After that, a small roller (like one used to paint walls) is dipped in a thick, oil-based ink and run by hand over the wax paper. Plain paper placed under the wax paper is thus imprinted with the words. A skillful printer can print five hundred copies from each piece of wax paper.

The technique was invented in Europe in the mid-nineteenth century and was favored by European socialists. In the 1920s and 1930s, the Chinese Communists learned it from the Russians, and used it to print in secret under the nose of the Nationalist government. Many stories of Communist heroes and martyrs described how they spread their message to the masses through such printed pamphlets.

During the Cultural Revolution, large, powerful factions seized official printing presses and use them to print materials favorable to their point of view. Smaller factions or individuals operated with wax paper printing.

I had mastered the technique in 1968 when my parents sent out hundreds of letters in their effort to secure an appeal for my grandfather's case. I helped out then, and now I was helping a dissident group which soon accepted me as one of them.

Li Yizhe was the penname of a group of young—actually, a few were not so young—people who found one another during the turmoil of the late 1960s. There were four major writers: Li (Li Zhengtian), Yi (Chen Yiyang), Zhe (Wang Xizhe), and Guo Hongzhi, whose name was not represented in the pseudonym. Guo, born in 1929, was considerably older than the others. The rest had been students in 1966, while Guo was already a mid-level government official.

Among the four, Guo seemed to be the key figure. He came from a rich peasant family in Shandong Province and received a traditional education before joining the Communist military in 1947. In the early 1950s, he was sent to fight in the Korean War, and lost all of his toes in the freezing North Korean winter. Returning to China as a disabled veteran, he was rewarded with a job in the Guangdong Provincial Radio Station. When the Cultural Revolution began, he headed the propaganda department of the station, which was a rather important job in those days.

Guo loved ancient literature and wrote classical poetry as a hobby. Like many cadres in those days, he was targeted by the Red Guards for his "bad" family background. After that episode, he joined the rebel faction, where he met Li Zhengtian, another rebel activist.

In the midst of the turmoil, the two began to suspect Mao's intentions. They believed that the country had been dragged into a civil war for no good reason. They felt the suffering of the people. They became nonbelievers, and examined everything through this new prism.

When Li Zhengtian was released from prison in 1972, the two met and exchanged ideas. They decided to write them down. This gave rise to the earliest version of *On Socialist Democracy and the Legal System*.

One day in 1973, when Li was walking down the street, he heard a familiar voice calling his name.

"I believe you are Li Zhengtian."

It was Wang Xizhe, his comrade-in-arms in the rebel organization from years before. Wang, born in 1948, was then a junior high school student.

Smart, handsome and self-centered, Wang was brave and rather ambitious. His role model had once been Mao. During the Cultural Revolution, it was fashionable for young students with traditional names to change them and adopt new ones with more "revolutionary" flavor, just as street names were changed during that period. Girls, for example, often named themselves *Hong* ("red"), or *Weihong* ("defending the red"), or *Dong* ("east"), after the last character in Mao's name.

When Wang and his schoolmate—later his wife—fell in love, he suggested she adopt the name Jiang, after Mao's wife. It was a telling request.

Although still in his late teens, Wang was one of the best writers among the rebels. Extremely eloquent and very well read (at least by the standard of the time), Wang often compared himself to heroes in Communist history. The first time I met him, he was telling the story of Louis Auguste Blanqui, a French revolutionary who had inspired the Paris Commune in 1871.

"Blanqui spent thirty-eight years in prison. I am prepared to spend thirty-nine!"

Later, he was jailed twice. The first time he was incarcerated for less than two years; the second time it was for twelve years, as a political dissident. At that point, he was a twenty-five-year-old who had just completed five years' labor on a farm, and was starting a new job in a fish processing plant.

Factories and farms were full of well-educated and ambitious young men and women during this era. This is hard to imagine today. Even in China, those people today would be in leading positions in business, government, academia, law, and the news media. In those days, however, they were laborers with ordinary jobs. But their status did not stop them from thinking about someday changing the nation.

When Li and Wang met, they felt an instant bond. Wang became part of the writing group, and he brought along his best friend, Chen Yiyang.

A quiet, meticulous, and humble young man of twenty-seven, Chen was ambitious in his own way. He had a genuine passion for history and philosophy, and dreamed about writing books on those subjects. (He did, years later.)

The four formed a writing group. They wrote all the articles under the name Li Yizhe. Guo's name was not represented, since he did not want to create the appearance of an older man manipulating the young, but they were equal partners. A final version of *On Socialist Democracy and the Legal System* was posted in public in November 1974. It was known as "the Li Yizhe poster."

Thousands of people sent in letters of support. Hundreds sent in plain paper, mostly anonymously. The printing system operated by volunteers like me produced thousands of copies of the poster. They were distributed through private channels—friends and friends of friends. Some of them produced more copies on their own. Within a few months, the poster became very well known across the entire nation. It was a very rare occurrence.

Centered around the four writers, two dozen people, most of them young, formed a group. We gathered once or twice a week, exchanging ideas and books. One of our favorites was a translation of Friedrich Hayek's *Road to Serfdom*. Hayek's overall criticism of the planned economy was extremely eye-opening. The other one—a long, hand-copied article—was Ota Sik's *The Third Way: Marxist-Leninist Theory and Modern Industrial Society*. Sik, a Czech economist, was a key figure in the Prague Spring. He promoted a market economy and served as Alexander Dubček's deputy prime minister. Milovan Djilas's theory of the new class criticizing the new privileged party bureaucracy also spoke to our hearts.

Writing about these authors, I realize that, with Communism disappearing from the face of the earth, some of their names are also fading from memory. Dissident writers from the former Eastern Bloc, like Solzhenitsyn, Sik, and Djilas, influenced millions of minds and contributed decisively to the demise of the entire Communist system. Li Yizhe was following in their footsteps in China.

Over the years, I have met many famous and smart people in many countries. Some of them participated in the governance of big countries like China and the United States; some planned conflicts like the Iraq War; some established themselves in law, academia, science, and other fields and achieved worldwide fame. I can testify that this small group of dissidents in southern China was no less brilliant than any of these big names. When resources were extremely limited, when information was controlled by the government with an iron fist, and when free thinking was a capital offense, they reached the conclusion that democracy and rule of law were the right prescription. I am extremely proud to have been associated with them—as their youngest member, in fact.

More important, our group was not an isolated case. Millions of young people who should have been in college had been "sent down" to the bottom of the social ladder, but hard manual labor did not stop many of them from learning and thinking. Paradoxically, the harsh reality—especially the politics and the severe poverty—caused them to think all the harder and to search for alternative solutions to their country's problems. China's future leaders, the best and the brightest in the nation, were reading and writing, even in the fields and factories in which they found themselves at this point.

Once I asked my students at UCLA to imagine an eighteen-year-old girl—me—who had only three years of formal education, reading a Chinese translation of Plato's *Republic* sitting next to an old machine at 3 a.m. during a short break in the night shift at my factory. It was not in fulfillment of any homework assignment nor in pursuit of any kind of career advancement, but purely for personal knowledge. The image was somewhat mind-boggling for them. But I was not alone. My like-minded friends and I were all searching for directions the nation might follow in order to emerge from its misery. We were looking for answers from all available sources—an extremely limited universe—to guide us to a brighter future.

Among these like-minded friends, I did not need to hide my thoughts anymore. I grew, I matured, and I finally became myself. I also found a love I had been longing for—a mother figure.

Li Xiufang, a historian, spoke with a beautiful Beijing accent, which was rare in Guangzhou. Everyone in the group called her "Big Sister Li," but I called her "Aunt Li," since, at forty years old, she was almost my mother's age.

Aunt Li had graduated from the history department at Zhongshan University and married a talented historian and writer. Her husband had been imprisoned in 1968 under military rule. After being humiliated on stage several times, he committed suicide by jumping out of a window. Aunt Li, an editor at the Guangdong Radio Station, was sent to do hard labor for four years and did not come back to the city until 1972. She occupied a small one-bedroom apartment, which was quite a luxury for a single person in those days. She had been a very close friend of Guo, and provided the group with a gathering place that afforded a measure of privacy.

I liked her the second I met her. A group of us—four or five—arrived in her apartment. She greeted us warmly, and asked:

"Have you eaten?"

Since we had not, she immediately went to cook something up in the kitchen. My grandma had raised me as a proper Chinese young lady, so I followed her and started to help. Later I learned that she always offered food to visitors, a most generous act during those years when food was so tightly rationed.

Soon I learned that Aunt Li was the glue that kept the entire group together. She provided them with a quiet place to gather and to write; she took care of everyone when they needed her; and she even offered up her small apartment as a print shop at one point.

One day, she led me into her windowless bedroom and pointed at bookshelves with hundreds of books. "Borrow any that you want," she said.

I was in heaven.

Aunt Li's late husband had loved the theater, so they had collected many books of plays: Greek tragedies, Shakespeare, Molière, Arthur Miller, Eugene O'Neill, etc. I read them all. I cannot even begin to describe the joy I felt. More than three decades later, I can still recite many of the lines by heart.

Aunt Li discussed the books with me each time I saw her. We shared our passion for tragedies, but not the comedies. The tragedies, especially those of Shakespeare, appealed to us a great deal, perhaps because of the deep sense of history we felt when we read plays such as *Hamlet* and *Macbeth*.

There were some women in the group, but most of the members were young men in their twenties who worked in factories. Since I was the youngest and a girl, I was often given minor duties, such as collating the printed pages or preparing tea or meals. I didn't mind a bit.

Every minute of my spare time was spent at Aunt Li's place, reading or helping out. I was more than happy to contribute in whatever way I could. I really felt that the more I gave, the more I received.

My heart and my mind were finally aligned. To me, our group was a vessel for a just cause.

Figure 8. Members of the Li Yizhe study group, circa 1975. I was not present at the time the picture was taken. In the center, wearing a cap. is Li Zhengtian; Wang Xizhe is at the far right.

Figure 9. Three of the founders of the Li Yizhe study group. From left to right, Wang Xizhe, Chen Yiyang and Li Zhengtian. The picture was taken in early 1975. Soon after, Li and Chen were both deprived of their urban residency and sent to do physical labor in remote areas.

STORY TWENTY-ONE: HEAVEN AND EARTH

If there is coordination between heaven and earth, and between the divine and the worldly, one cannot find better evidence than the string of melodramas that occurred in 1976.

After almost ten years of political turmoil, the entire nation had entered a stage of profound disillusionment. The senior Communist leaders who had founded the Party in the 1920s were getting old. Everyone knew they might die soon, regardless of how many times "Long live Chairman Mao" was shouted. Mao, born in 1893, was already 82. Each time he showed up in the news, he looked more frail. He could utter only broken sentences that could barely be understood by anyone except his young nurse, who was rumored to be his mistress. Therefore, the "supreme instructions" in Mao's last years were full of grammatical mistakes. Although they were laughable, they nonetheless had to be closely followed.

On December 16, 1975, all radio stations in China broadcast the same piece of music, the official mourning dirge that would become far too familiar to the Chinese people in the year to follow. On that day, one of Mao's extremist cohorts, Kang Sheng, had died. Kang was widely loathed for his leading role in the persecution of moderates inside the Party.

Three weeks later, the radio broadcast the same tune. This time it was for Premier Zhou Enlai.

Zhou was a complicated figure. He was without question the smartest and shrewdest of the veteran Communists. He had followed Mao closely—closely enough to prevent himself from falling from grace like so many others. But he had also kept a distance from Mao and his cohorts, enough to make people believe he was a moderate. People had seen him as the symbol and the hope that China one day would return to some level of normalcy.

It was a cold and dreary winter day. I was riding my bicycle to work when I learned the news. Immediately, I switched direction and went to Aunt Li's house.

Guo Hongzhi was already there, as were a few other members of our group. The leader of the moderate faction was now gone. What would the future bring? Would China keep advancing toward even more repression, as Mao's "continuous revolution" suggested? Would angry people around the country finally rise up? Would such a showdown come soon? Would it take the form of a bloody war? If so, what should we, as a group, do?

Deep in our hearts, we were convinced China would experience a civil war after Mao's death. We were children of war. Some of us had participated in it, and all of us were prepared for it. From day one, the Communist regime had been telling the people that the country was surrounded and infiltrated by enemies. A war would be inevitable, it had warned.

Somehow, we were always psychologically prepared for war. I was in love with a man in our group at the time. Once we halfheartedly joked about a possible common future—fighting a war together.

"I can be the commander in chief in the army," he said, "and you can be the commissar."

"I don't want to be a damned commissar!" I retorted. "I want to be the commander in chief!" But I wasn't joking when I said I was ready to die for the cause.

On the day Premier Zhou died, China was indeed on the verge of another round of turmoil.

"The heavens are angry, and the people are furious," Guo observed. And sure enough, soon after Zhou's death, Deng Xiaoping, the vice premier, was purged for a second time.

Deng had always been known to be a very practical person. After the disastrous Great Leap Forward, he had repudiated its political extremism in a famous observation: "It doesn't matter what color a cat is; as long as it catches mice, it's a good cat." He proposed to apply the same principle to the economy, and encouraged limited market reform. From 1956 to 1966, he had been the general secretary of the Party. During the Cultural Revolution, he had been condemned as "the number-two capitalist roader," after Liu Shaoqi. He was tortured by the rebels and put under house arrest. His eldest son, a student in the Physics Department of Peking University, was publicly humiliated and fell—or perhaps jumped—from a fourth-floor window, which caused him to be paralyzed from the waist down. His brother committed suicide.

After Lin Biao's death, Deng returned to power and became the vice premier. When Premier Zhou fell ill with cancer in 1975, Deng took charge of the economy. He tried to implement pragmatic policies, such as reinstituting the bonus system in factories, allowing better workers to earn a little more and giving the peasants a little more freedom to plan their tiny private gardens and sell excess products on the open market. In February 1976, he was accused, again, of promoting capitalism, and lost his power a second time.

This time, the people were furious—not at Deng, but at Mao and his cohorts. In March, spontaneous demonstrations, held in the guise of honoring the memory of Zhou Enlai, sprang up around the country. Railway workers in Nanjing posted slogans supporting Deng Xiaoping on trains, and thus spread the word around the country.

Beijing's Tiananmen Square quickly turned into the center of the demonstration. Thousands of demonstrators—perhaps two million at the peak—gathered on the square. Demonstrators read poems and posted articles, criticizing Mao and his wife. Some vowed to use violence against the dictators. When a small group of policemen arrested dozens of demonstrators, the angry mob destroyed a few police vehicles and burned police headquarters.

The police and the militia then moved in, drove the demonstrators away with clubs, and arrested hundreds of them.

When government radio broadcast the news and condemned the demonstration as "a counterrevolutionary riot," we could somehow sense that the end of the Mao regime was near.

But what would be next?

The supernatural forces of heaven—if there were any—seemed to give a hint. On May 29, two earthquakes measuring 7.3 and 7.4 on the Richter scale occurred in Yunnan Province. Ninety-eight people died. What was significant from a political point of view was the name of the place in which the earthquake occurred: Longling County, which translates as "County of the Dragon's Tomb." The dragon, of course, was the traditional symbol of the emperor.

It was a coincidence that turned even some confirmed atheists into believers. Rumors flew around the country. Some suggested Mao was already in a vegetative state, while others placed Deng in hiding somewhere, protected by his friends in the military. The government ordered the police to arrest anyone who spread such news. Rallies were held to denounce the rumors, which of course made them even more interesting to people already hungry for information.

On July 6, the radios again broadcast the official dirge. It wasn't for Mao, though. It was for Marshal Zhu De, the ninety-year-old Communist military veteran who been out of power for a while but who had managed to retain his prestige. Mao was still alive—barely.

People whispered that perhaps Mao was a "true dragon" who must take many people with him when he left this world. Would there be more deaths?

Such a worry unfortunately became reality on July 28, when another earthquake—this one a 7.8 on the Richter scale—took almost a quarter-million lives in Tangshan, a city north of Beijing. The entire city turned to rubble in just a few horrible minutes. The nation seemed paralyzed by the tragedy. If there was a God, he must surely be very angry with the Chinese.

September 8 marked the Mid-Autumn Festival, the second-most important holiday on the traditional Chinese lunar calendar. I was working the evening shift that day. I went to the rooftop with a dozen fellow workers during the meal break. We shared our food and moon cakes—the traditional pastry associated with the holiday—and enjoyed the full moon as usual.

The moon was shining brightly in the dark blue sky. It was a typical September night in this tropical city. Rain fell mostly during the afternoons, cooling the air, making evenings rather pleasant.

"Look!" A colleague suddenly pointed at a corner of the sky.

A small, dark cloud shaped like a spear was floating slowly toward the moon. In a few minutes, the cloud closed up and appeared to cut into the center of the moon. Slowly but steadily, it expanded, blocking the moonlight for a while.

"Clouds over the moon during Mid-Autumn Festival—this is not a good sign," a fellow worker in her fifties murmured.

The next day, Mao passed away.

The mourning theme from the radios permeated every corner of the city. The music of death. Everything and everyone seemed to stop moving—buses and pedestrians on the street, machines in the factories, and teachers and students in the schools. By order of the government, the entire country was decorated with white flowers and black cloth, making the world seem entirely black and white.

I went to Aunt Li's place that evening. Several members of our group had already arrived. One of them said, "Finally, it happened. We have been waiting for it for too long."

Even among this group, this was a very bold comment. No one dared say any more. To voice such an opinion was still a capital offense.

We looked at each other, speechless.

What would be next?

STORY TWENTY-TWO: PRISONER IN MY HOUSE

In the years since I had gotten a job, I had grown into a total stranger to my parents. I regularly worked six days a week, plus overtime on half of the Sundays. I would leave early for the night shifts and come home late from the day shifts. Eventually, when the factory began to provide beds for single workers—one for every two people, so we had to take turns—I stayed away as much as I could. I was happy; I had friends, a job, and a clear purpose in life.

I wrote about my new friendships and shared my work with the dissident group. I put all my heart into it, and could not bring myself to destroy my own writing. Yet it was not safe to leave my diaries in my bed in the factory, since someone else from another shift was sharing it. I kept them under my bed at home. If I was home, I stayed in my bed, which was on the top bunk. That was my own realm. Since my schedule shifted often, my parents did not pay much attention.

That was until one day in 1975, when my parents summoned me. Mother was holding a bunch of my writings in her hand.

My heart sank. I felt dizzy. I was frozen in place.

She stared at me furiously, shouting, "What have you done?! What kind of friends have you been making?! You are shameless! You are such a slut! I always knew that about you!"

She showered me with insults, repeatedly accusing me of being sexually promiscuous, based solely on the observation that most of my friends were male.

Indeed, I had written passionately about my love for a particular young man. But I wasn't sexually active. Frankly, at that point the idea had never even crossed my mind.

Standing there listening to her, I gradually became defiant. I said calmly, "I don't think that you are qualified to judge me." I had no intention of giving in.

She slapped my face. I did not move.

The next day, Mother went two places. First, she stopped by my factory to see the Party leaders there. She gave them all my writings and asked the factory to withhold my wages. Her reasoning was that since I might use my money to support counterrevolutionary activities, it was in the state's interest to give the money to her, so that she could control my expenditures. She also volunteered to provide them with details of my day-to-day schedule. If I was missing for a few hours, I would surely be participating in antigovernment activities.

Next, Mother stopped by the home of the man I loved. Luckily, he was not home. She screamed at his parents and warned them never to let me set foot in their home or see their son again. Otherwise, she threatened, she would report their entire family to the police.

It was the end of any possibility of reconciliation with my parents, especially my mother.

The Party leaders in my factory agreed to give my wages to my parents, but they were not thrilled with Mother's proposal of how to constrain me. My factory was a small and unimportant work unit. I was a good and productive worker. A little bookish, perhaps, but harmless. Other than my political thoughts, I was trouble-free to them. In an era when young workers were fleeing to Hong Kong and many other kinds of troubles dominated their agenda, the Party leaders did not relish the idea of more work. After all, how much damage could the thoughts of an eighteen-year-old on Plato or Hegel or Hayek—ancient and foreign names of whom they had never heard—do to the Party? None of the leaders had ever finished high school.

The leaders nonetheless summoned me to their office the next day. They told me about my mother's visit, and informed me that they would be giving my wages directly to my mother from then on. Then they warned me not to make the wrong kind of friends, and let me go.

I went to see the forewoman of my shift. She was a kind lady in her late thirties. I asked her to assign me more overtime.

"Why? You have already been working very hard!"

"I need the money."

I really did need the money. And I knew that overtime pay was not handed out as part of one's wages, and would still be given to me directly. I wanted time away from home. I could see my friends during meal breaks. Aunt Li's place was less than ten minutes away by bicycle. If I worked two consecutive shifts, I could get a one-hour meal break.

Therefore, one and half shifts became my regular schedule. Mother could not stop me; if she had tried, I could have accused her of preventing me from working hard for the state. She gave me back half of my wages for meals, which was far from enough.

I was young and energetic, but even so, a twelve-hour work day was a little too much. I began to fall asleep in the middle of my night shift. One night at 3 a.m., while I was repairing the machine, perhaps half-asleep, I suddenly felt a sharp pain in my left hand.

The glove on that hand had been swallowed by the moving parts in the machine. I looked at my hand and saw blood shooting out of my middle finger. Immediately, I wrapped it in my apron and ran to the door.

"What happened? What happened?" three of my fellow workers yelled, chasing after me. When they saw the blood, they ran with me to a hospital only ten minutes away. A small portion of my finger was missing.

I acquired a little more freedom after that incident. Still claiming I was working overtime, I spent more time with friends. Perhaps convinced that I was hopeless, or perhaps tired of being my watchdog, Mother dropped her project of keeping tabs on my schedule.

In the summer of 1975, Zhao Ziyang, the provincial Party secretary who had prevented the arrest of the Li Yizhe group, was sent to be Party secretary of Sichuan Province. His replacement was Wei Guoqing, a known hardliner. He had been the chief Chinese military consultant to the Vietcong during Dien Bien Phu in 1954. After coming back to China, he was appointed head of the Guangxi Zhuang Autonomous Region, partly because he was of Zhuang (one of China's minority ethnic groups) origin. During the Cultural Revolution, Wei had been attacked by local rebels, but he eventually triumphed, becoming the only provincial head in the nation who had never lost his position, even for a day. He launched a brutal counterattack against the rebels, which resulted the death of thousands—or perhaps as many as a hundred thousand, according to some researchers.

Immediately after Wei replaced Zhao, Li Zhengtian and Chen Yiyang were detained and deported to remote areas to do hard physical labor. Li was sent to work in a mine, and Chen to a farm. Every known member of the group received a warning.

I got my warning from the Party leader of my factory. But I did not really care. After all, I had nothing to lose except my friends, and I knew I would never abandon them.

STORY TWENTY-THREE: REVERSAL OF FORTUNE

The country seemed to cease operating after Mao's death, which was par for the course after the death of a supreme leader. Nothing was "normal" any more. For a while, the nation felt leaderless, regardless of the fact that a successor handpicked by Mao, Hua Guofeng, was in place. Hua commanded neither the authority nor the prestige of the dead, paramount leader. He was weak—something you could even tell from his dull expression. Hua vowed to "continue Chairman Mao's revolution," but the nation, by contrast, was waiting for major change.

Although the media revealed nothing, its rhetoric soon tilted subtly away from the political tone set by Mao. My sixth sense told me that something was cooking, something powerful. What would that be? Would it be more turmoil caused by a power struggle? Or would it be the release from the political pressure cooker for which the nation had long been waiting?

The rumor mill was the most effective news medium at the time. One month after Mao's death, some shocking news came out of Beijing.

On October 13, I was working my evening shift. During the meal break, I went to Aunt Li's house. She was away, but a group of us still gathered there regularly.

A friend revealed what he had learned from his contacts in Beijing: a coup d'état had occurred a week before. Mao's widow and three of her cohorts—later called the "Gang of Four"—had been arrested by military leaders who supported the moderate faction, and who were friends of Zhou Enlai and Deng Xiaoping.

In other words, four weeks after Mao's death, his legacy was being thrown off the political stage.

It was the end of the Mao era. Everybody understood the importance of the change. But would it also signal a reversal of fortune for us? More importantly, would it presage a new era for the nation?

It turned out that the Gang of Four had been arrested on October 6. That same evening, the Party leaders who had launched the coup, many of whom had suffered during the Cultural Revolution, decided first to take over the Radio and Television Bureau, through which they would control the broadcast media. It seemed that their intention was to leak the news quickly but steadily instead of keeping it a secret. People working for the Bureau called their friends. The friends called other friends. Within two or three days, the well-connected in Beijing—reporters, government officials, and college professors—all knew about the coup. Within a week, the news had spread throughout China's larger cities.

This was crab season in Beijing. In a not-so-veiled reference to what had occurred at the highest levels of government, local crab vendors were hawking four crabs on one string, shouting, "Good catch! Three males and one female!"

Millions of people celebrated spontaneously on the streets. Drums and Chinese firecrackers broke the deathly silence that had followed Mao's death. Children and adults marched together, laughing and smiling, suddenly liberated from the relentless pressure of Mao's "continuous revolution."

I was marching with my fellow workers, and a thought crossed my mind: perhaps university admission would once again be open for competition? Might I have an opportunity to change my life? Oh, how much I wanted to go to school! I was thirsty for knowledge.

On October 21, two weeks after the downfall of the Gang of Four, the official media finally reported their arrests and the nation celebrated.

It was quite a dramatic reversal of fortune, not only for the power holders themselves, but also for millions of people who had been persecuted during the previous years and who were expecting vindication.

Sidney Rittenberg, an American Communist who had come to China in 1945 and joined the Chinese Communists, had become a leading activist at the Broadcast Bureau, the place where he worked. In 1968, he had been arrested. Accused of being an American spy, he was jailed in the infamous Qingcheng Prison, where high-ranking Communist leaders were incarcerated from time to time when they were out of favor. Rittenberg was in Qingcheng for almost ten years. In the early 1990s, when I met him at Harvard, he described a dramatic episode. One day in 1977, he heard hysterical screaming from a cell across the hall.

"Oh, Chairman Mao, I will always be loyal to you! I am forever your soldier!"

He recognized the distinct female voice. It was that of Mao's widow, Jiang Qing.

"I immediately thought: if she was in, I ought to be out soon," Rittenberg told me. And indeed, he was released within days.

Deng Xiaoping came back to power in May 1977. He became the paramount leader of the Chinese Communist Party in December 1978, although he never took a formal title that would indicate this. This time, he would hold on his power until his death in 1997, and he would transform China into a very different country. It was the beginning of the Deng era.

My aunt was released from prison. One day in July 1977, the party leaders in the military hospital for which my Aunt once worked invited my grandma in. They told Grandma:

"Your daughter made a mistake when she was sentenced. But we recognize that the sentence was unreasonable. She will be out soon, and we will again accept her as one of our own. She should be grateful. She will get her rank and salary back, as if the past eleven years never happened."

"Never happened" was the exact phrase used by Party leaders in millions of such cases.

Grandma, not wishing to jeopardize her daughter's chances of release, said nothing. In fact, it was lucky her daughter had even remained *alive* during eleven years of torment.

The military took my aunt to a halfway house. She had weighed 120 pounds when she was taken; at the time of her release, she was only eighty pounds. The military fed her decent food for a week, and then led her into an office.

Her divorced husband—still not remarried and raising their two children—was waiting in the same room. The Party leaders informed them that the state would regard their divorce as something that had never happened, and that she should report for duty at her old post within a few weeks. Finally, the Party leaders pointed at a table in the room:

"Here is your money."

On the table, there was a large stack of money—my aunt's salary for the previous eleven years. Without counting it, the couple stashed the money into a large tote bag and immediately went home.

Many cases proved that the halfway houses were an absolute necessity. After years of imprisonment and torture, some poor souls could not stand the excitement of exoneration. Many had strokes or heart attacks on the spot. Celebrations turned into funerals. My friend Yang's father was jailed for fifteen years. In February 1979, he was released and exonerated. He was so thrilled that he died of a massive heart attack.

"Release the good news bit by bit to prevent sudden death," instructed a directive from the central government in 1979.

However, in the fall of 1976, when the Gang of Four had just been arrested, few people expected such dramatic turnarounds. In fact, the reversal of fortune was slow to gain momentum. A large-scale exoneration campaign did not begin until late in 1978. Before that, there were a few more campaigns of persecution. More people would fall into the political meat grinder established by the Communist Party.

Chen Yiyang, one of the Li Yizhe writers, had predicted as much when he heard the news of the downfall of Mao's widow:

"The new regime may persecute a large number of people just to establish its authority. We may yet have another round of terror," he warned people in our group who were celebrating, including me. He was the most coolheaded of all of us, perhaps because of his personality or his family background; his father had been an important Nationalist officer in the 1920s, and was constantly targeted under Communist rule. It was second nature to him not to trust the Communist leaders, moderate and radical alike.

Unfortunately, his prediction proved accurate.

In the first few months of 1977, hundreds of thousands of people were arrested or detained around the country, alleged to have acted as "forces of turmoil under the Gang of Four." Supporters of the Gang of Four, political dissidents, and rebel activists during the Cultural Revolution who once targeted Party leaders were all considered in the same category. Some of them were soon executed, including well-known Shanghai dissident writer Wang Shenyou, who had openly declared that Mao was not a Marxist. He was put in front of a firing squad on April 27, 1977. (Three years later, the government recognized him as having been "a martyr for the socialist state.")

On March 2, 1977, the four major writers of the Li Yizhe group were arrested. In the next few weeks, more than thirty others who had participated in the activities of this group were detained, including me. It was apparently not yet our turn for a reversal of fortune.

STORY TWENTY-FOUR: FREEDOM WITHIN

I was taken to a small cell near my factory on the third floor of a warehouse. The cell had been set up for the sole purpose of locking me up. Seven female guards—all selected from the factory workforce, since my work unit had to pay all the costs associated with my persecution—were assigned to watch me day and night, two per shift. They were ordered not to talk to me, except to respond to my requests for bathroom breaks and to bring me food three times a day.

Within the first hour, two men had come in and installed thick wooden crossbars on the only window in the room, reducing my view of the outside to a dozen small, square holes about the size of my fist. This was a standard procedure, since it was not uncommon for people to jump out of windows during their detention.

"Don't worry. I have no intention of committing suicide," I said to the guards. They ignored me.

I was taken in the afternoon. Four people came to see me that evening, lead by the stranger in the old military uniform who had first showed up when I was detained. Later I learned that his name was Chen. He was a bureau chief in the provincial police department who had been put in charge of the Li Yizhe case.

Chen informed me that the Public Security Bureau had created a task force to investigate my case. The three other people who showed up with him—all women—were part of the task force. How many others there were, I had no idea. They were all to work full-time on *me*.

"The party and the state are expending a lot of resources to save you. You should be grateful," I was told.

Right. As if I had asked for it.

I must have had a look of defiance on my face. He continued:

"We are giving you three days to think things over. Then tell us if you regret what you have done."

During the next three days, I did think things over. I did not have anything else to do anyway—I was permitted no books, no newspapers, and no one to talk to.

It was a strange, reflective time. Since I had met my dissident friends almost three years ago, my life had been a string of exciting events. I had made many friends. I had fallen in love. And I had participated in activities that were branded as taboo. But I had never sat down and had a conversation with myself about the meaning and purpose of my own life.

Everything around me was eerily quiet. A small bed, a table, and a few chairs filled the tiny room. The Guangzhou sky—rarely blue—was sectioned into small squares by the barred window. When the sunlight shone through, the squares would create spots and shadows, making the dusty, depressing furniture look more colorful. I could hear the guards chatting from time to time, and traffic somewhere out there. It was a different world, the world of outside.

During the first few days of my incarceration, in the tranquility of my small cell, I began coming to terms with myself, with who I had become.

I imagined my life without the past three years, without friends, and without all the activities the Party considered not only sinful but criminal. What would it have been like? Then I remembered the days before that time—a life without much meaning, an empty heart, no one to talk to, and nothing to live for. I concluded that I might just as well have been dead.

Although I was in trouble because of politics, I was actually not fond of politics. I had no desire to be part of any political power, and no ambition to perform for the public. I wanted to be neither a hero nor a villain. I simply longed to be left alone by the authorities—of whatever kind—and to be myself.

I wanted my freedom *from* politics, not *in* politics. On top of that, I desired a few opportunities to read more, to learn more, and to see a broader world beyond my home and my factory.

I imagined school, friends, and love. I imagined limitless amounts of books, no boundaries to knowledge, no fear of speech, and no barriers to friendship. In my mind's eye, I would have all these things someday. Did such desires make me a bad person? No, I didn't think so.

Actually, on reflection I came to be proud of myself. I compared my life with those of others around me. I was not yet twenty-one, but I had already broken a lot of the boundaries drawn around me by the government.

I just missed my friends terribly. In such an environment, all my senses seemed to be heightened, and my feelings intensified. I knew that my friends, too, were all locked up. I went through all the details of our relationships in my mind. Spiritually, at least, I was with them.

Three days seemed very long with all those thoughts going through my mind. I had neither calendar nor watch, and I was denied newspapers. In isolation, each day felt like months. Fearing that I might lose my mind if I did not keep track of the actual date, I started to carve lines on the wall, each line representing one day. It became a ritual in the first hour of every morning, until I had drawn 110 lines. At that point, I had become accustomed to life inside and did not care anymore.

Three days later, my interrogator came back.

"I know that you all have some models to follow. I have been thinking who my model should be. I have to say, I envy no one," I told my interrogators three days later.

No one? They seemed not to believe their ears.

No one, I confirmed.

They were surprised by my answer. One of them said:

"If you behave yourself and confess your crimes, we will let your parents see you."

I almost screamed, "No!" My parents! I had almost forgotten them. For heaven's sake, they were the *last* people I wanted to see! Suddenly, I realized why I hadn't been feeling too bad about being locked up. My parents were not around. That, at least, gave me some measure of freedom.

The interrogators showed me a stack of paper. I saw my mother's handwriting and read the first page. According to Mother, I had shown signs of not being a good person very early on. When I was three years old, she had taken me and my sister—only a year older—to a gathering. Someone asked:

"Which one is the first?" The questioner meant the first-born.

"This one." Mother pointed at my sister.

I began to cry: "I am the first! I want to be the first!" Mother said this clearly indicated how selfish I was.

It was laughable. I didn't want to read any more, and threw the paper back at the interrogators. "I am not interested in reading more condemnations," I said.

I was too inexperienced to anticipate what would happen later. It seemed that the special team assigned to my case did a very thorough investigation of my associations with other people, and had questioned each of them, especially my friends in the Li Yizhe group. They also seemed to understand my defiant and stubborn personality.

They closed in on me slowly. First, they asked me about the details of our group activities—who presented in which meeting, what they said, and what they did. It seemed that they already knew a lot. Well, most of those "meetings" were simply casual gatherings of friends. No one would have considered them secret at the time.

Every day, for a few hours, my case officers would interrogate me. Sometimes the interrogation would run for more than ten hours. Unwilling to make things easy for them, I intentionally supplied them with misinformation. For instance, I would insist that some people had not been present at certain meetings, or that I did not remember certain things having been said. I thought that I was helping my friends, until one day—

twenty-eight days after I was put in that cell—my interrogators came in with a very large stack of written materials.

"You made a lot of trouble for us," one of them said. "We had to check with each one in your group. We know you have been playing with us."

They read me a few paragraphs from a few of my closest friends. Those accounts detailed some of the meetings I had insisted never happened.

I suddenly realized that I had been making a great deal of trouble for my friends. The authorities were methodically putting everything together to make cases against them. Our group had never tried to reconcile our stories with one another, since we did not regard our activities as criminal. Any misstatements from me meant that my friends would be interrogated more intensively.

"If you are incarcerated, it is better to tell the truth," I remember Aunt Li once telling me. She had been imprisoned a few times during the Cultural Revolution.

Mindful of that, I began to recall the details. And the more details I recalled, the clearer the picture of our activities I had in my mind became. I realized that the people in this group had come together for no purpose other than expressing and exchanging ideas. Such ideas were all within the scope of Marxism, since we had no other influences on our thinking.

I demanded a copy of the four-volume *Selected Works of Marx and Engels*. I said I needed the books to refresh my memory, since so many of the conversations my interrogators were asking about were discussions about Marx and Engels. They finally gave me the books, two months after I had been put in that cell.

Over the next eight months, I memorized every word in those volumes, including the footnotes and the index pages. (Years later, I could still amaze my classmates at Harvard by reciting those articles verbatim.)

Those volumes saved, if not my life, then surely my sanity, because right before that time, I had experienced my first "struggle session."

Such rallies were techniques used by the Communists in every political campaign. They were designed to publicly humiliate their victims, to torture them psychologically and physically, and to isolate them further from their families, friends, and the public.

That day, I was put onstage in front of perhaps a thousand people, mostly co-workers from my factory. A long banner was hanging in the back of the hall, which read:

"You must surrender; otherwise you are doomed!"

Looking at all the familiar faces in the audience, I felt I was doomed anyway. Standing on the stage, I was convinced that the end of my world was near.

I cannot remember who gave the introduction. But the next thing I knew, half a dozen of my co-workers in the factory mounted the stage, one after another. Each of them made a speech denouncing me.

In their prepared scripts, there were things about me that were most private. They cited conversations I had had with other co-workers at work to prove my "reactionary thoughts." They quoted my love letters to show my "bourgeois sentiments." (Those materials supplied by Mother finally proved their usefulness.) It was a devastating blow to a twenty-one-year-old.

I tried to control my emotions. I had too much pride to show how hurt I was. If there was any comfort to be had, it was in the attitude of some of the speakers. They read from the scripts without any feeling, a clear signal to me that they were not willing participants in the charade.

The session lasted for two hours. Within three or four months, seven such rallies were held. After two or three times, I got used to it. Hell, millions of people had had the same experience under Communist rule. I wasn't alone. If other people had survived, I could, too.

By the fall of 1977, everything seemed to quiet down. My interrogators rarely came. When they did, they showed little desire for more information. My guards began to talk to me, and brought me newspapers. Deng Xiaoping and many high-ranking officials who had lost power during the Cultural Revolution returned to power. I was also informed that my aunt had been released after eleven years of imprisonment. The world seemed to be changing.

The most shocking sign of change came at the end of 1977, when the government announced that university admission would be reopened to public competition. All high school graduates beginning with the class of 1966—the year in which *yje* universities were closed—would be allowed to compete.

It was the first time I regretted what I had done. Why hadn't I held on for a few more years? If I had, I would have had the opportunity to compete now! I would actually have had a future!

I wept, again and again, at night. Someday I would be let out. But with a label like "counterrevolutionary," my future was ruined forever.

One of my guards was a year older than I was. She was preparing for the examination and brought her textbooks with her. One day, she walked in and showed me a mathematics problem.

"Do you know anything about this? I have no clue," she said.

Mathematics wasn't my best field, but in all those book-hungry years, I had studied all the old high school textbooks on my own. I took a quick look and solved the problem immediately.

After that, she switched to the evening or night shifts whenever she could, and brought the books into my cell when no one was looking. We studied together. Actually, I tutored her. For some reason, academic subjects always came very easily to me.

I was sure that if I had the opportunity to take the exam, I would excel in it. But I was locked up in this tiny cell. My tormentors seemed to have forgotten me.

I wished they would all rot in hell. The Party, too.

STORY TWENTY-FIVE: MY WAY OUT

In March 1978, I was released from my cell. There was no resolution, no sentencing, and no apology. My interrogators simply told me:

"You have lots of reactionary thoughts. However, we have decided that we might be able to reform you. Go back to work in your factory."

Being marked as someone to be "reformed" indicated that I would not be formally sentenced, at least not in this case.

Political change was coming, slowly but steadily. More and more purged officials came back to power. Some classic books, Chinese and Western alike, began to appear in bookstores. Textbooks were suddenly widely available. At universities, new undergraduates— their ages ranging from as young as fourteen to as old as thirty-two—studied for their own futures, and for that of the nation. Hope was in the air.

Both my sister and brother achieved good scores on the college admission exam, left home, and entered universities. In my brother's case, his admission was delayed, and he was admitted to a school far lower on the scale than his scores would have permitted. Later, he was told that his political background was the cause of this misfortune, since he had a sister who was in government custody. My other kid brother was slated to graduate from high school and sit for the exam soon.

My parents took me back with great dismay. They repeatedly told me that I had shamed the family and that I deserved even more punishment. My co-workers were ordered not to talk to me beyond what was absolutely necessary. Every day, they politely said hello and stayed away.

I felt lonelier outside than inside. Everyone treated me as if I had some kind of dreaded infectious disease. I could feel our neighbors pointing me out behind my back as a negative example for their children.

I dreamed about my friends. Many of them had been released like me, but we could not see one another without risking another round of persecution.

Human kindness, even under such conditions, shined through from time to time, however. On one particular day, my co-workers held a celebration at a local restaurant to mark an across-the-board raise in wages. As expected, I was not invited. The next day, my forewoman grabbed me quietly in the morning, and said:

"Come with me at lunchtime."

I did. She led me into the warehouse, where no one was watching. As if she were a magician, she produced a dish of food and said: "We saved this for you from yesterday. Eat. No need to say anything."

I realized that my co-workers had actually saved the best bits of meat for me. I could not find the words to thank her. As she had said, there was no need.

Eyes filled with tears, I ate the meal.

In the summer of 1978, another round of college admission exams was held. Later, when the exam questions were released, I decided to test myself. Realizing how easy they were for me, I became more depressed. I began a systematic study of China's ancient history. The Chinese had kept records for four thousand years. These were available in libraries and bookstores now. History showed that even during the conservative periods, things were always changing. I sensed that a major change would come my way very soon. I just hoped it would come soon enough to give me a chance to go to school.

In the second half of 1978, the new Party leadership in Beijing was apparently deviating even further from Mao's political line. In November, the 1976 Tiananmen Square protest was officially vindicated. It was now being referred to as "the people's great protest against the Gang of Four." All 388 protestors who had been sent to jail became national heroes.

The major reform came in December 1978, when the Eleventh Central Committee of the Chinese Communist Party held its Third Plenum. Mao's successor, Hua Guofeng, was compelled to perform a self-criticism and was forced to hand over power. The new paramount leader, Deng Xiaoping, urged the nation to engage in a "liberation of thought" campaign. Mao's theory of continuous revolution officially ceased to be the guiding principle behind Party policy. A massive campaign of exoneration—covering everyone from the rightists of 1957 to the millions persecuted during the Cultural Revolution—was underway. Finally, after so many of its own had been victimized, the Communist Party had tired of its own vicious cycle, and had more or less come to its senses. It would no longer actively seek large-scale persecution, at least not as often as had occurred during the Mao years.

A new Party secretary, Xi Zhongxun, was assigned to Guangdong. Xi himself had been persecuted more than once, and imprisoned for a long time. He was known to be sympathetic to the victims.

One day in October, one of my friends from the Li Yizhe group stopped me outside my factory. My heart melted at once; I had found my friends again. Beginning in October 1978, members of the group began to contact one another again. After the Tiananmen Square verdict, we became more confident that our turn for exoneration would come very soon. Even then, the four principal writers remained in jail.

On December 30, all those remaining in prison were released.

The security cadres in my factory informed me of the news. With smiles on their faces, they said I would be welcome if I stopped by their halfway house, a famous hotel in the city. It was hard to believe that these were the same people who had detained me twenty months earlier.

Immediately, I rushed to the hotel on my bicycle.

Most of the people in the group were already there. We laughed and shook hands. Men embraced one another. It was a time of great celebration.

Li, Chen, Wang, and Aunt Li looked familiar, but I did not recognize a thin man. With his wispy, grey hair, he looked to be in his late fifties. I was wondering who this guy was when he started coming toward me. From his limp, I recognized that it was Guo; he had lost all his toes during the Korean War. He was sixty pounds lighter than he had been two years before. The only familiar things about him were his witty smile and his old-fashioned glasses.

Xi, the provincial party secretary, met with the entire group a few days later. He looked like a kindly old guy. When we complained about our persecution, he sighed:

"I was imprisoned several times, too—sixteen years altogether."

Although he had joined the Communists in the 1920s, he had never been jailed by the Nationalists, only by his own comrades. I could not imagine how someone who had experienced such persecution could remain a loyal Communist, but apparently many people did.

In February, the provincial Party Committee organized a rally to exonerate the Li Yizhe group. We were hailed as heroes for daring to criticize the Gang of Four, although I remembered that we had criticized much more than just them.

Exoneration rallies would also be held in each victim's work unit. Since the government had humiliated them publicly, it was only appropriate that they be vindicated publicly. It was the ritual of the time. Sometimes, a long list of names—of people dead and alive—would be read aloud at such rallies. For their part, victims were required to attribute all of their suffering to the Gang of Four, although many of the killers or torturers were, in fact, sitting right there in front of them. They were also required to thank the Party for "liberating" them, and to praise the greatness of the Party.

A rally was held in my factory to exonerate me, as if I cared.

My speech must have set the record for brevity. I stood on the stage and said, simply, "This is over. Let it be over."

After that, I sank myself wholeheartedly into my textbooks, preparing for another round of exams, which would come in July. A whole new future was potentially waiting for me to grab.

On July 7, 1979, I sat for the three-day college admission exam, and five weeks later, I got my news. I had received the highest score among the two hundred thousand others in my province who had also taken the test, and as a result was admitted to Peking University, the most prestigious in the nation. I chose to study history, my favorite subject.

STORY TWENTY-SIX: WE, THE JAIL BIRDS

Beginning in the fall of 1978, all known dissident groups around the nation tried to establish a network. This was part and parcel of what has been labeled the "Democracy Wall" movement.

In February 1979, the Li Yizhe group received a letter from a group calling themselves "the Beijing Spring." The selection of such a name was clearly influenced by the Prague Spring. A group of young people who had participated in the Tiananmen Square protest in 1976 and who were referred to as the "Tiananmen heroes" by the press had established this organization in Beijing. They published a magazine—also named *Beijing Spring*—an act that was unprecedented in Communist China.

The letter congratulated us on our exoneration, and invited us to participate in a discussion in the magazine about how to build a democratic system in China. Li Zhengtian replied to the letter, expressing our joy and willingness to participate.

In September 1978, two months before the Tiananmen Square protesters were officially exonerated, a magazine named *China Youth* published a collection of the poems posted by the protestors. The magazine belonged to the Communist Youth League, and had been closed down during the previous decade. This was the first issue to be published after the Cultural Revolution.

The magazine did not pass the censors, and was banned. But on November 15, someone posted the contents of the banned publication on a wall in downtown Beijing. Thus "Democracy Wall," as it was later called, was born. It lasted for a year. Dissidents from all over the country came and posted their articles. Every day, hundreds of thousands of people squeezed their way into the crowds, reading and hand-copying the articles. Copies were quickly distributed to the readers, who greedily absorbed every word.

The degree of freedom was unprecedented, but the freedom was far from unlimited. In March 1979, Deng Xiaoping ordered the arrest of a dissident named Wei Jingsheng, who had posted one article demanding more democracy and written another criticizing Deng as the "new dictator." Wei was later sentenced to fifteen years for "revealing state secrets," for he had allegedly discussed some military movements with foreign reporters.

Our group had received the letter from the Beijing Spring group at the time the sky looked the brightest. A few people in our group corresponded with them. So when I received the admission from Peking University, Li Zhengtian wrote a letter to the Beijing Spring.

"We have a comrade who is going Peking University. Please tell us how to contact your comrades when she arrives."

The Beijing Spring group quickly answered:

"When your comrade arrives, she should go to Building No. 39, Room 105, and ask for Comrade Wang Juntao."

These are literal translations. The word "comrade" was genuine, since we considered ourselves comrades-in-arms in the fight for democracy. The language and terminology remained somewhat Communist in style, even though we all knew that we were in a new era and had engaged in anti-Communist activities. Some habits die harder than others. So the first person I met in Beijing was another jailbird. Wang was two years younger than I was. A handsome and shy young man, he had been a high school student in 1976 when he led his classmates to protest in Tiananmen Square. He was arrested and jailed for a few months. In 1978, he took the college admission examination and was accepted by the Department of Nuclear Physics at Peking University. Almost all of his colleagues in the Beijing Spring group—also his prison comrades—won their spots in various universities in the same year. Like many in my generation, China's baby boomers, they had struggled all the way back to school from farms, factories, and military camps.

On New Year's Eve of 1980, the History Department held a party. Dozens of students attended. Some of us were in our early thirties, some in our late teens, and others in between. We introduced ourselves—where we came from, what we had done, etc. All sorts of odd job titles popped up, among them mechanic, janitor, farmer, needleworker, shepherd, military cannon operator, barefoot village doctor, and even a village Communist Party secretary.

We realized that among ourselves we actually had enough diverse experience to run the country, professionally speaking. (And I may add that many of those history students *are* running the country now).

Even having "imprisonment" on one's résumé was not all that rare. Cao, a graduate student at the Department of Law, had been one of the leaders of the 1976 Tiananmen Square protest. At the time, he worked in the office of China's official trade union. He had led twenty-seven of his colleagues on a march to the Square on the morning of March 30. This was the first act of the protest. He was later arrested. When he was released a year later, his case officer quietly told him that he had been on the list of nine people who would have been sentenced to death, had Mao's death not occurred first.

The most astonishing story I've ever heard belonged to a student at the People's University. Li, a young worker in Wuhan, had joined a small dissident group in 1974. They gathered privately to discuss the problems and the future of the nation, just like my group did in Guangzhou. The next year, the government found out. The most senior person—a twenty-four-year-old worker—was sentenced to death. Li, only nineteen at the time, received a death sentence with two years of probation—the law said he was too young to be executed. Two years later, he was released and won college admission.

Those tragic years were behind us now, we hoped.

Naturally, students like me studied very hard. The magnificent library, the sea of knowledge, and the multiplicity of ideas ... my life had already been enhanced beyond my wildest dreams.

And somewhere along the way came the idea of going to America. In the early 1980s, American universities started to invite more and more Chinese scholars to visit, and the Chinese government agreed to send a small number of students to study abroad, mostly to America. In the mid-1980s, students at Peking University learned that American universities provided scholarships to qualified foreign students. TOEFL—the standard U.S. test of English as a foreign language—became the hottest game at school. A Chinese translation of William Manchester's *The Glory and the Dream: A Narrative History of America, 1932–1972* was among the most-read books on campus. Arthur Miller's *Death of a Salesman* was the most popular play in town. And

American history was one of the most sought-after subjects in my department.

Two American teachers at Peking University helped shape my view of the United States and whet my appetite for study in America. In 1980, the Fulbright Program sent a history professor to lecture in my department for two weeks. He gave each of us a copy of *Democracy in America*, the timeless masterpiece by Alexis de Tocqueville. I read every word of the book over the next two years, but could understand only a little. That was the first English book I ever read from cover to cover.

My knowledge of English was also greatly advanced by my association with another American teacher, Sue Bremner, who is now a senior diplomat in the State Department. She was then a young graduate student from Berkeley who had accepted the challenge of teaching English in China. From the readings in her class, I memorized two sentences from the Declaration of Independence that I feel are arguably the most important fifty-five words in modern history: "We hold these truths to be self-evident: That all men are created equal; that they are endowed by their Creator with certain unalienable rights; that among these are life, liberty, and the pursuit of happiness; that, to secure these rights, governments are instituted among men, deriving their just powers from the consent of the governed." I dreamed about America often. To me, America was everything China was not, and especially had not been during those horrific decades of the '60s and '70s. The liberty, rule of law, and democracy enjoyed by the American people seemed to me to be heaven-sent. And the character of the Americans—humorous, adventurous, independent-minded, yet collectively well-organized—captured my fancy. I could easily picture myself living happily among such people. When I read American history and American literature, I felt a strong sense of kinship. More than anything, I wanted to go there.

So I started at the top. Why not, after all? I applied to several of America's most famous schools. I had good grades from college, and several of my professors wrote strong recommendation letters. In my application, I briefly summarized my experiences: never finished elementary school, worked on a farm and in a factory, was a dissident and got into trouble, and finally earned a BA and an MA from Peking University. Amazingly, Harvard, Yale, and Columbia all gave me offers of admission, and eventually I accepted admission and a fellowship from Harvard.

It all felt strangely easy. Harvard did not ask me to vow that I was politically loyal to anyone or any party. It conducted no check on what kind of family I came from, or whether any relative had ever gotten into political trouble. No one seemed to care. For the first time in my life, I felt that it would be fine to just be me. Actually, it would be more than fine. It would be great.

On April 24, 1987, I landed in Boston. Finally, I was in America, where I had always belonged. It had only taken me thirty-one years to get there.

Figure 10. With friends at Peking University in 1987, just before I left for the United States. All of them are established scholars now.

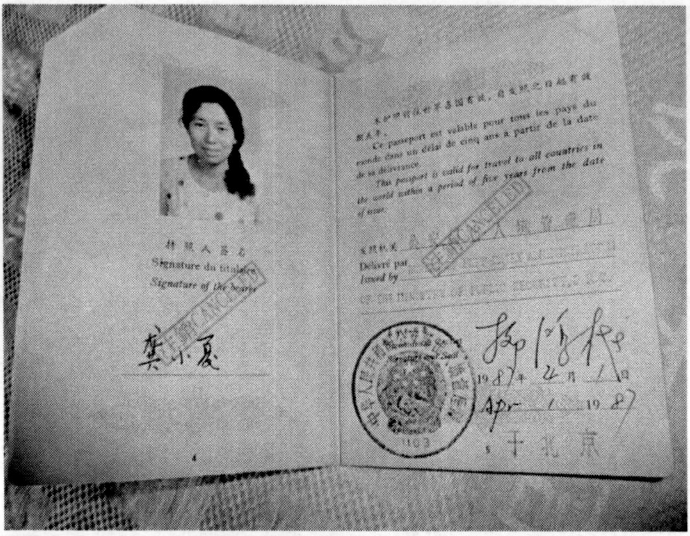

Figure 11. My Chinese passport, issued April 1, 1987.

Figure 12. My first July 4 in the United States, in 1987. This photo was taken in front of the Massachusetts State House in downtown Boston.

Figure 13. Graduation from Harvard University, 1995. This was taken right after the ceremony. Yunxiang Yan (left) was my schoolmate at both Peking University and at Harvard. We were married at the time. We remain very good friends.

EPILOGUE: BECOMING AMERICAN

On June 4, 2003, I was fired from my job at Radio Free Asia for insubordination, after I repeatedly protested the unfair treatment of the Asian employees there. Asian immigrants counted for more than 70 percent of the employees, but all but one of the thirteen senior management positions were filled by non-Asians. The immigrants also earned far less than non-immigrants doing comparable work, and were given little opportunity to advance to executive positions, although some had a lot more experience and knowledge of Asia and more years of education than those who held the senior jobs.

The company sent me a letter of termination while I was on vacation. Somehow, my boss, with whom I had raised the equity issue repeatedly, could not bring himself to do it face to face.

My termination was reported in the press, both because my name was somewhat well known in the Chinese community and because Radio Free Asia existed in the world of media.

One Chinese, driven, no doubt, by deep-felt, ultra-nationalistic feelings, learned of the news and sent me an e-mail message that read, "Pro-American Chinese like you, who have sold out the motherland, should learn a good lesson from this. Now the Americans betrayed you. You deserve it."

I replied, "Sir, I believe that you are misunderstanding my situation. I am not *pro*-American. I *am* an American. This is my country, too."

I took my boss to court and sued the company, accusing it of racial discrimination and retaliation. My American friends teased me that the lawsuit signaled that I was truly beginning to behave like an American. And I promised myself that I would fight the battle like a real American.

Radio Free Asia hired a top Washington law firm, Hogan & Hartson, to represent the company. I found a lawyer in a small law firm fighting for human rights and labor rights. A classic David and Goliath battle. And not totally unexpectedly, David won. The company asked to settle the case after only three depositions. I was actually having some fun during my own deposition when the company lawyers questioned me for eleven hours, hoping to wear me down. It all felt like child's play compared to the endless interrogations, deprivations, and struggle sessions I had experienced at the hands of relentless Communist interrogators with nothing else to do but try to break my spirit so many years before. In the end, I came away with a $450,000 settlement and a strong sense of vindication.

But while I was glad for the vindication, I ultimately did not really feel like either a victim or a winner, but rather a citizen. More than anything else, I felt American.

I believe that the most important ideas about America, the ideas of the founding fathers, were not about the Goliaths, but rather about the Davids, and about their God-given rights to life, liberty, and the pursuit of happiness. Davids from all over the world built this nation. They enjoy equal rights and equal protection under the law. They may not have many possessions or much money, but they all have this country.

Since becoming an American citizen, I have been very active in community organizations. I donate to them and volunteer for the causes in which I believe. During the past few elections, I have volunteered time to help get out the vote, especially among Asian-Americans. As I once told a reluctant voter, "Please vote. I don't care which party you vote for. This is a right I once went to jail for. Don't give it up easily." And, of course, I always vote myself.

Over the years, I have thought a great deal about my two cultural identities. I was born in China and lived there for thirty-one years before leaving for the States, where I have been for twenty years. Am I more an American, more a Chinese, or some sort of hybrid? There is no question about my political allegiance, since few would willingly choose dictatorship over democracy. But how about my cultural identity? Do I think, behave, and believe more like an American, or more like a Chinese? At its heart, what, ultimately, is my identity?

My conclusion is that, paradoxically, living fully as an American has allowed me to be *more* Chinese than ever before. The more I identify as an American, the prouder I am of my Chinese heritage.

Chinese culture dates back five thousand years. Its longstanding values and morals have nurtured one of the greatest civilizations in human history. China's Confucian culture promotes social mobility based on education and merit. It requires people to be virtuous, humble, reasonable, and compassionate. It places a great value on loyalty within the family and between friends, and stresses harmony between human beings and nature. And it strongly condemns brutality, dishonesty, and government arbitrariness.

Once, Confucius was asked to summarize the most important human virtue. He answered: "Never impose on others what you would not choose for yourself." Such principles have guided the Chinese in the construction of their society, and helped them rebuild it many times after disasters.

These basic values have been severely damaged during China's half-century experience with Communist rule. In a few short years, traditions five millennia in the making were thrown out the window and smashed beyond recognition. Political dictatorship causes distrust among people and between people and the government. When people have no power, they don't feel any responsibility. The dictatorship thus produces an irresponsible, disaffected citizenry.

When I rebelled against Communism, I was also protesting the damage it had done to my culture and my national traditions. I wanted to be the person my grandma had taught me to be—honest, humble, and compassionate, always opening my heart to fellow human beings who needed me. I wanted to be a person governed by the *best* of the Chinese traditional virtues.

I feel free to be just such a person in America. I can embrace my heritage without worrying that the authorities will come to smash it. I can be warm, open, and honest with my fellow citizens without constantly watching my back. And I can express my opinions publicly without fear of going to jail.

The difference is not between Chinese and American, but between bondage and freedom, dictatorship and democracy, brutality and humanity. Here in a free, democratic society, under the protection of the law, I can be Chinese and American at the same time.

Here in America, I am home.

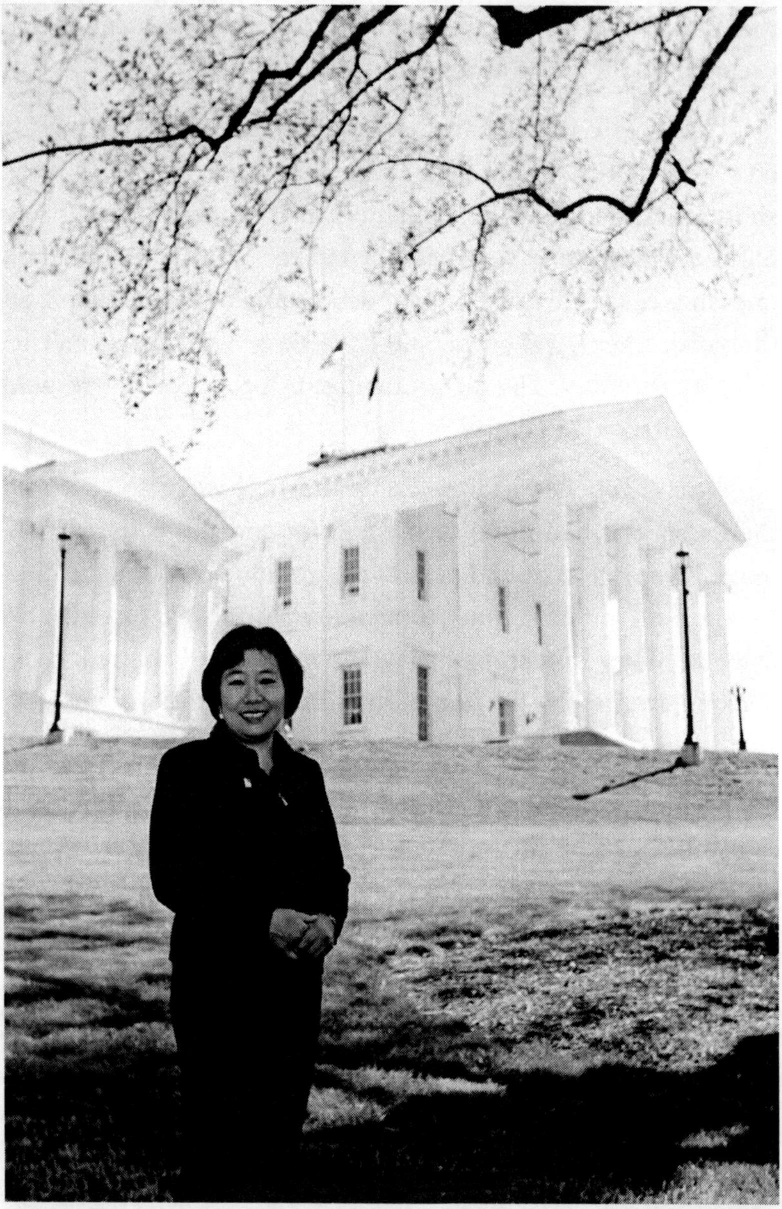

Figure 14. In front of the Virginia State House, Richmond, Virginia, 2009.

Figure 15. Washington, D.C., 2009.

APPENDIX I: CHRONOLOGY OF CHINA IN THE TWENTIETH CENTURY

1911	**The military officers and Nationalist leaders overthrew the Qing Dynasty. The Republic of China was founded.**
1917	The Russian Revolution. The Russian Bolsheviks seized power.
1921	The Chinese Communist Party was founded in Shanghai with the support of the Russian Bolsheviks. Mao Zedong was among the founders.
1927	The Nationalists started a massive persecution of the Communists. The Communists held peasant uprisings in the south and established a small Red Army.
1931	Japan occupied Manchuria.
1935	The Red Army accomplished an eight-thousand-mile-long march, and established a new base in the north. Mao overwhelmed the Soviet-backed factions and became the paramount leader of the Communists.
1937–1945	Japan invaded China. The Sino-Japanese war lasted for eight years. The Nationalists worked with the Communists during the war.
1945–1949	A civil war between the Nationalists and the Communists broke after the end of World War Two. The United States endorsed the Nationalist government.
1949	The Communists took over mainland China. Mao declared the founding of the People's Republic of China on October 1.
1950	Millions were killed during the Land Reform campaign. Landlords were deprived of land ownership.
1950–1953	The Korean War.

1956	The campaign of collectivization and nationalization established the state and collective ownership of land and industries.
1957	The anti-rightist campaign persecuted millions of intellectuals.
1958	The Great Leap Forward campaign aimed at rapidly raising industrial and agricultural production.
1959–1961	A great famine was caused by the Great Leap Forward, in which twenty to forty million people starved to death.
1965	The "Four Cleansing" campaign, the prelude of the Cultural Revolution.
1966	The Cultural Revolution was launched by Mao. The chaos began with Red Guards persecuting teachers and the "bad classes." Soon, Mao's political rivals within the party were also persecuted, especially by the rebels.
1968	The military took over after two years of chaos and civil war between factions of mass organizations.
1970	The One-Attack and Three-Anti campaign was launched with massive arrests and execution.
1971	Mao's deputy Lin Biao led a failed coup d'état, and was killed in a plane crash on his way to the Soviet Union.
1972	Nixon went to China. Deng Xiaoping came back to power.
1974	Mao launched the "Criticize Confucius and Lin Biao" campaign.
1976	Premier Zhou Enlai died in January. Deng Xiaoping was ousted the second time. Large-scale protests occurred around the country, including the one in Tiananmen Square. Marshal Zhu De died in July. Tangshan Earthquake killed 240,000 on July 28. Mao died on September 9. Mao's widow Jiang Qing was arrested on October 6.

1977	The CCP declared that the Cultural Revolution was finally ended, and reinstalled the college admission exam system. Deng Xiaoping again came back to power.
1978	The Third Plenum the Eleventh Central Committee of the Chinese Communist Party was held. Deng Xiaoping became the paramount leader. A massive exoneration campaign began to clear victims of the previous political persecutions.
1979	Deng Xiaoping visited the United States. "Special economic zones" were established in two southern provinces, Guangdong and Fujian, as pioneers of the economic reform.
1979–1989	Economic reform was underway, but political dissidents who criticized the Communist party were still persecuted.
1989	Millions of people joined student protesters in Tiananmen Square, demanding democracy and political reform. On June 4, the military moved into the Square, killing many protesters along the way. Premier Zhao Ziyang lost his power after the crackdown.
1992	Deng Xiaoping made a series of speeches in his trip to southern China, urging the continuation of the economic reforms. China adopted a market-oriented economic system.
1997	Deng died on February 19.

APPENDIX II: CHRONOLOGY OF SASHA GONG

June 1956	**Born in Beijing to parents who were faculty members of the Beijing Normal University.**
Oct. 1956–Sept. 1961	Raised by Grandma in Guangzhou, Guangdong Province.
Sept. 1961–Aug. 1962	Attended kindergarten in Guangzhou.
Sept. 1962–Aug. 1965	Attended elementary school in Guangzhou.
Sept. 1965–Nov. 1965	Attended elementary school in Changsha, Hunan Province.
Nov. 1965	Grandfather was accused of being a counterrevolutionary and lost urban residency.
Nov. 1965–Jan. 1966	Stayed with grandparents in a village in Hunan Province.
Jan. 1966–Dec. 1966	Stayed with great-aunt in a small rural town in Hunan Province, when the Cultural Revolution was launched.
Jan. 1967–Oct. 1969	Lived at home in Guangzhou, when the civil wars between factions were ongoing.
Oct. 1969–Aug. 1972	Worked in the countryside building houses or working in farms half of the time; stayed home the rest.
Sept. 1972–August 1979	Was a production worker in a candy factory.
1974	Was involved in the Li Yizhe dissident group.
April 1977–March 1978	Was detained for participating in counterrevolutionary actions.
March 1978	Was released from detention.
March 1979	Was exonerated.

July 1979	Took the college admission examination.
Sept. 1979–June 1983	Studied for a bachelor's degree in the Department of History at Peking University.
Sept. 1983–June 1986	Studied for a master's degree in the Department of History at Peking University.
April 1987	Arrived in America.
1988–1995	Studied for a PhD at Harvard University.

INDEX

LaVergne, TN USA
15 January 2011
212612LV00005B/4/P

9 781934 840900